Taking Sides: Clashing Views
in Childhood and Society, 11/e

Kourtney Vaillancourt

http://create.mheducation.com

ISBN-10: 1259910911   ISBN-13: 9781259910913

Contents

Detailed Table of Contents

Unit 1: Infancy

Issue: Does Maternal Employment Have Negative Effects on Children's Development?
Yes: Patricia M. Anderson, Kristin F. Butcher, and Phillip B. Levine, from "Maternal Employment and Overweight Children,"
National Bureau of Economic Research (2002)
No: Daniel de Vise, from "Study: Working Mothers Not Necessarily Harmful to Child Development," *Washington Post* (2010)

Researchers Patricia M. Anderson, Kristin F. Butcher, and Phillip B. Levine from the National Bureau of Economic Research conclude that there is a connection between maternal employment and the risk of children being overweight. Daniel de Vise describes the results of a study conducted at Columbia University, which indicate that the negative and positive effects of maternal employment balance each other out to yield a neutral effect.

Issue: Should Parents Be Allowed to Genetically Engineer Their Children?
Yes: Antonio Regalado, from "Engineering the Perfect Baby," *MIT Technology* (2015)
No: Akshat Rathi, from "The Pros and Cons of Genetically Engineering Your Children," *Quartz* (2015)

Antonio Regalado urges caution in, but does advocate for, moving forward with genetically engineering children, discussing some of the existing ethical and moral concerns that scientists have identified. Akshat Rathi reports on the conclusions of a meeting of minds regarding the practice of genetic engineering. Their conclusion is that we neither know enough about safety issues or how humans will respond to such practices to condone them.

Issue: Are Transracial Adoptions Problematic for Children?
Yes: Darron T. Smith, from "Can Love Overcome Race in Transcracial Adoption?" *Huffington Post* (2013)
No: Jessica Ravitz, from "Transracial Adoptions: A 'Feel Good' Act, or No 'Big Deal'?" *CNN.com* (2010)

Darron T. Smith presents evidence from research that indicates that transracial adoption is not problematic for children. Jessica Ravitz argues that transracial adoptions do not have to be problematic for children. Jessica Ravitz argues that transracial adoptions do not have to be problematic for children but does identify potential challenges that may be faced.

Issue: Is the Achievement Gap Increasing in America?
Yes: Sabrina Tavernise, from "Education Gap Grows between Rich and Poor, Study Say," *New York Times* (2012)
No: Rebecca Klein, from "Schools Are Finally Starting to Embrace This Method of Closing the Achievement Gap," *Huffington Post* (2016)

Sabrina Tavernise reports on U.S. studies that show the education gap is growing between the rich and the poor. Rebecca Klein identifies a new method that schools are using in order to close the achievement gap.

Unit 2: Early Childhood

Issue: Is Spanking Detrimental to Children?
Yes: Rupert Shepherd, from "Spanking Children Can Cause Mental Illness," *Medical News Today* (2012)
No: CTV.ca News Staff, from "Contentious Study Says Spanking May Benefit Children," *CTV News* (2010)

Rupert Shepherd discusses findings from the American Academy of Pediatrics that state spanking can cause children to have an increased risk of mental problems as they age. CTV News Staff reports on a study that argues children who are spanked might grow up to be happier and more productive than children who are not spanked.

Issue: Are Fathers Really Necessary?
Yes: Gail Gross, from "The Important Role of Dad," *Huffington Post* (2014)
No: Mary Riddell, from "A Child Doesn't Need a Father to Be Happy," *The Guardian* (2007)

Gail Gross discusses the important functions that dads fulfill for their child(ren). Mary Riddell discusses that while fathers can be valuable, there are circumstances in which it is actually favorable for a child not to have a father in their life.

Unit 4: Adolescence

Lori Rose Centi addresses the differences in male and female brain development, and how gray and white matter in the brain can impact adolescent behaviors. She also discusses other brain changes that may contribute to males being more impulsive and less careful than their female peers. The Frances McClelland Institute shares a fact sheet which dispels "myths" about the differences in male and female teens. It reports on a meta-analysis of 148 studies and the resulting major findings. Different types of aggression are defined and discussed.

Chandra Johnson describes some of the harmful effects that the Internet can have on teenagers. Lauren Sherman advocates for more research to be conducted before a firm determination is made about the impact of the Internet on adolescents.

Stopbullying.gov defines cyberbullying and the potential effects it can have on victims. It also discusses the frequency of cyberbullying, according to recent studies. Nick Gillespie acknowledges that bullying occurs but argues that there are other issues that parents should be more concerned about. He discusses some of the reasons he believes that people have become so sensitive to bullying, and how it may be impacting parenting strategies.

Rachel Ehmke identifies several risks associated with teenage social media use. Peg Streep identifies some of the needs of teenagers that social media can fulfill.

Preface

When I was in college, I majored in family and child science. A large emphasis of my major was child development. I learned the most important theories, talked about the latest strategies for dealing with problems children face, and generally feel like I gained a solid understanding of childhood and society. There was a lot to read and so much that I wanted to know more about. By the time that I graduated, I believed that I was well informed about the most current information that was coming from the research. I was also opinionated and was sure that I knew what children need in most common situations. Then, I had children of my own. My husband and I waited what is generally considered a long time before we had children, so I was a little older than many of the other new moms that I interacted with. My age, along with my education, helped me to feel confident that I would make the best choices possible about the upbringing of my children. To a certain extent, this was true. However, I have to say that my boys have challenged me from the beginning, even before they were born! Becoming a parent made me consider (and re-consider, and re-re-consider) issues from different perspectives, in ways that I had never really thought about. The things I had previously discussed only as abstract notions now became personal. Should I immunize my children? Do I let them watch TV and movies? What happens if they are bullied? All of these questions that I previously could answer with "facts" became much muddier when I was thinking about them in terms of my own children.

This book is intended to encourage the reader to consider differing perspectives on issues that children and families face today. For each of the issues addressed, a pro and a con perspective based on research is provided. I encourage you, whether you are a parent or not, to carefully consider the cases that each author makes. Personalize the material, ask yourself what you would tell a parent or caregiver about these issues. Or, ask yourself what you would do if it were your child. You may find yourself agreeing with one side or the other, or you may find that your opinions fall somewhere in between the two sides. The outcome is not important; there is merit to each side of the argument. What is really important is that you allow yourself to consider differing perspectives and are able to apply it to your future professional work and family life.

Kourtney T. Vaillancourt, PhD
New Mexico State University

Editor of This Volume

KOURTNEY T. VAILLANCOURT, PhD, is a college associate professor of family science at New Mexico State University in Las Cruces, NM. She is a licensed marriage and family therapist and drug and alcohol abuse counselor in private practice, clinical member, and approved supervisor of the American Association for Marriage and Family Therapy. She received a BS from New Mexico State University, an MS from New Mexico State University, and a PhD in family studies from Virginia Tech. She edits a bimonthly newsletter for AAMFT's Approved Supervisors, and she edits *Taking Sides: Clashing Views in Childhood and Society*, which is in its tenth edition. And, she is wife to Steve and the proud mother of two fine young men, Etienne (8) and Emerick (6).

Acknowledgments

I would like to thank Lindsey Trujillo for assisting with the 11th edition of this book. I also want to extend a warm thanks to Jill Meloy, Senior Product Developer.

Academic Advisory Board Members

Members of the Academic Advisory Board are instrumental in the final selection of articles for each edition of Taking Sides. Their review of articles for content, level, and appropriateness provides critical direction to the editors and staff. We think that you will find their careful consideration well reflected in this volume.

Celcilla Alvarez
San Antonio College

Janine Bempechat
Wheelock College

Christopher Boe
Pfeiffer University

M. Jennifer Brougham
Arizona State University

Leilani M. Brown
University Of Hawaii–Manoa

Rebecca S. Carothers
Ivy Tech Community College of Indiana

Chris Carreira
Henry Ford Community College

Sandra Collins
Brown Mackie College

Nancy DeFrates-Densch
Northern Illinois University

Lee Doebler
University Of Montevallo

Kathleen E. Fite
Texas State University–San Marcos

Josephine Fritts
Ozarks Technical Community College

Bernard Frye
University of Texas, Arlington

Caridad Hernandez
Florida National College

MJ Hubertz
Florida Atlantic University

Ronald E. Lewis
Grand Canyon University

Lawanna M. Lewis
Grand Canyon University

Dennis A. Lichty
Wayne State College

Lewis Lipsitt
Brown University

Dean Meenach
Mineral Area College

Bradley Morris
Grand Valley State University

George Muugi
Kutztown University

Caroline Olko
Nassau Community College

Jessie Panko
Saint Xavier University

Michael Patte
Bloomsburg University

Laura Pierce
University of West Alabama

Guillermina Raffo Magnasco
Broward College

Doug Rice
California State University, Sacramento

Stefi Rubin
Wheelock College

Thomas R. Scheira
Buffalo State College

Stephen T. Schroth
Knox College

Hilary Seitz
University of Alaska–Anchorage

Leretta Smith
North Dakota State University

Monica Sylvia
Le Moyne College

Chelly Templeton
Palm Beach Atlantic University

Anthony Teri
Union County College

Valerie Wallace
California Lutheran University

Introduction

Childhood can be a wondrous time when days are filled with play and new discoveries, nights provide rest and security, and dedicated, loving parents nurture their children and meet their needs. Some children do indeed experience the full joy of childhood; however, regretfully, there are other, more sobering scenarios: There are children who do not have nurturing adults to guide them, who go to bed hungry and some who do not even have homes. Most typically, childhood experiences fall between these two extremes. So there is a wide variety of experiences that can impact the developing child, and larger social forces are at work as well. Ask yourself as you debate the issues in this book the extent to which society must collectively address and resolve them. This is a vital function of society because children are society's future.

To understand and appreciate children in contemporary society, it may be useful to briefly review how society's views of children have changed over time. Most child development texts review the history of adult perceptions of children in western European society. Would it surprise you to know that in ancient times children were sometimes killed as religious sacrifices and buried in the walls of buildings? People believed that this practice would strengthen a building's structure. Up until the fourth century, parents were legally allowed to kill their newborns if the children were not in good health at birth. They were also permitted to do away with a child if they already had too many children, if the child was female, or if the child was illegitimate. In 374 a.d., the Romans outlawed infanticide, hoping that this would end the killing. Since parents could no longer legally kill their children, unwanted infants began to be abandoned. This practice endured for more than 1,000 years. It was not until the 1600s that child abandonment was outlawed throughout most of Europe.

During the seventeenth century, foundling homes were established to provide for the needs of unwanted children. During this period, children were considered to be miniature adults. They were dressed like adults and were expected to act as adults would act. By contemporary standards, parents took a rather casual attitude toward their children. This was probably due to the high child mortality rate at the time. Since parents thought it likely that their children would die in infancy or childhood, they did not get as emotionally close to their young children as parents typically do today. It was not until the end of the century that society began to look upon children as different from adults.

Early in the 1700s, European societal attitudes about children underwent further change. Children were no longer considered to be miniature adults, and literature written specifically for children began to emerge. By the end of the century, children who went to school were grouped by age, reflecting an awareness of stages of growth. The eighteenth century also marked the rise of the systematic study of children, which centered around the moral development of children and child-rearing problems.

It was not until the beginning of the twentieth century that three distinct age groupings emerged in the study of human development: infancy through age four or five; childhood to late puberty or early adulthood; and adulthood. This time period also marked the beginnings of the distinct field of child study. Early child study emphasized descriptive accounts of individual children and was mainly concerned with aspects of physical growth. As the century progressed, the term *child study* was changed to *research in child development*. Mothering became an important concept in the study of early child development, and the psychological aspects of development began to be examined more rigorously. Today, in the twenty-first century, research in child development focuses on issues related to family systems and the larger social issues that affect child development.

Nature–Nurture Controversy

There are many things that impact individuals as they progress through the human life cycle. People, places, events, illnesses, education, success, and failure—have you ever thought about the number of experiences each of us encounters in our lives? If one were to place all of the variables that influence human development into two general categories, those categories would be heredity and environment. As you may know, your genetic blueprint was determined at the moment of conception with chromosomes contributed by your father and mother. In a sense, for many of us, environment is also determined at the moment of conception. A good portion of the major elements of what makes up one's environment is often determined before a person is born. The society in which one will live, one's cultural and ethnic heritage, and one's family and subsequent socioeconomic status, for example, are usually predetermined for a child.

For this edition of *Taking Sides: Clashing Views in Childhood and Society*, I have selected articles that look at children in general and how they affect or are affected by the issues raised, rather than give you, the reader, clinical case examples of issues related to a certain child or children. For the purposes of this book, I make three assumptions: (1) When I discuss a child's environment, I am usually describing elements of the society in which a child is growing, developing, and otherwise being socialized; (2) all child development occurs within this social context; and (3) children cannot help but affect and be affected by the societal forces that surround them. In most university classes, students derive a certain sense of security in receiving definitions of terms that are used frequently in a given class. I offer the following one for *society*, which we have adapted from Richard J. Gelles's 1995 textbook *Contemporary Families*:

> Society is a collection of people who interact within socially structured relationships. The only way that societies can survive their original members is by replacing them.

These "replacements" are the children about whom the issues in this book are concerned.

Determining an appropriate group of societal issues and fitting them into the confines of only one work on children and society is a challenging task. Consider, for example, the diversity of contemporary society. We live in a sea of divergent and unique subcultures and ethnicities. Categorizing and describing the myriad values, customs, and belief systems of these groups could fill many volumes. In America and Canada, for example, there are many ethnic subgroups of citizens who are considered to be of Anglo descent, such as English, Irish, Italian, Polish, German, Greek, Russian, and Scottish. There are people of native descent, who are affiliated with scores of different tribes and subtribes. Some Canadian and American citizens trace their heritages to a variety of Asian countries, including China, Japan, Vietnam, Cambodia, Thailand, and the Philippines. Among blacks, there are those who trace their roots to the Caribbean region and those who identify with different regions of Africa.

In light of the foregoing, it may be reasoned that there are really no "typical" children in society! Although there are strong arguments supporting similarities within each of these general groups, there is a wide array of subgroupings and differences in customs and beliefs. As a consequence, when reading a book such as this one, it is important to be mindful of the extent to which differences might exist for those who may be of another race, ethnicity, religion, or socioeconomic status than the target group of children about which a selection focuses. It would also be prudent to consider geographic locale—rural, urban, northeastern, and southwestern—when considering the relevance of a given argument to a specific subgroup of children.

Children in Contemporary Society

It is worth understanding children's points of view as they are molded by society. It can be astonishing to take a step back and observe children as they undergo the socialization process in contemporary society. They come into the world totally helpless, unable to feed, care for, or protect themselves. As they grow and develop, children undertake the process of acquiring a sense of identity and learning the rules of the society in which they live. This process of socialization is fostered by many of the subsystems of society that provide prescriptions for behavior in particular areas of life. These subsystems include the family, the peer group, the school system, religion, and the media.

One important consideration is that up to about age five, children are oblivious to most racial, ethnic, religious, or socioeconomic differences. Typically, children can only realize differences in external appearance. One implication of this fact is that children can be much more amenable to learning and embracing a variety of cultural behaviors, attitudes, and even languages when they are young. Only as children move into middle childhood do they begin to recognize and understand other, more subtle differences. It is important to note that although young children may be oblivious to these differences, they are nonetheless impacted by them in the way they are socialized by their parents, families, and the significant others in their lives. This is done through family rituals, traditions, and outings; religious ceremonies; types of food prepared in the home; location where children live; and things that are found in the home, such as books, magazines, music, and so on.

Societal influences on children do not stop within the family system. As children grow, other institutions in society, such as schools, the economy, politics, and religion, expand their life experiences. Controversy arises as to how children react to these experiences. Consider, for example, what happens to children when both parents are employed outside the home. There are factions in our society who adamantly ascribe many of the problems associated with children to the fact that many parents are overly involved with work at the expense of time with their children. They contend that one parent (usually the mother) should stay home with the children, especially when they are young. Children who care for themselves after school and the quality of after-school childcare are also hotly contested, related issues.

Few readers of this book will be unfamiliar with the attacks on the mass media for its portrayal of violence in movies, television programming, and video games targeted at children. Again, researchers, clinicians, teachers, policymakers, and others fall on both sides of what should be done to address this.

As children move toward adolescence and become more independent, concerns regarding identity, values, morals, and sexual behavior become issues of controversy. Homosexuality, for example, which often is first evidenced by a person in adolescence, is considered by many to be a learned and abhorrent form of sexual expression. Others believe that there are people who are predisposed to homosexuality for reasons that are as yet unclear.

Events in contemporary society have a direct or indirect impact on children, despite attempts to protect them. Violence, inflation, war, poverty, AIDS, racism, and new technology are just a few of the phenomena that shape the society in which our children are socialized.

Researching Children

In finding answers to controversial topics, policy makers and the public alike often look to research literature for clues. The typical college student might think of researching a topic as going to the library or logging onto the Internet and looking up information on a subject, reading that information, formulating a conclusion or opinion about the topic, and writing a paper that conveys the student's findings. This is not the type of research about which I am referring! The type of research that I refer to here is called empirical research. This means that there is some question or group of interrelated questions to be answered about a topic. Data are then collected relative to the topic, and these typically shed light on how one goes about answering the question.

Data collection in research on children is undertaken from a variety of approaches. It could entail things like observing children at play in preschool or interacting with their parents at home. This is called observing children in a natural setting. With this method, observers must code

behavior in the same way each and every time it is seen. Most of the information we have today on physical growth and developmental stages was acquired through observation by child development pioneers such as Arnold Gessell and Louise Bates Ames. You can imagine how time-consuming this form of study must be.

Another type of data collection is called an experiment. Experimental researchers systematically control how certain things happen in a situation and then observe the results. In this type of research, an experimental group and a control group are chosen. Both groups are examined to determine that they are the same before the experiment begins. The experimental group then receives some kind of treatment, while the control group receives no treatment. Then, tests are conducted to see what kind of change, if any, has occurred between the two groups.

Interviewing children with a structured set of questions or giving children a structured questionnaire on a given research topic are other ways of collecting data. Projective techniques, where children might reveal their first thoughts about a picture or word, is also a form of the interview method.

The study of children can be organized in a variety of ways. One is by stages. The parts of this book (infancy, early childhood, middle childhood, and adolescence) are one type of stage organization. Another way to organize research endeavors is by topics. Topics are usually organized within the context of social, emotional, intellectual, physical, creative, and even spiritual aspects of development.

The time frames used to gather data on children also vary. In longitudinal data collection, information is collected from the same subjects over a long period of time. For example, one could examine the effects of preschool education on performance in elementary school by following and testing the same children during the preschool years and all the way through the elementary years. Because this type of research can take years to complete, a shorter method, cross-sectional research, could be used. In the previous example, one group of preschoolers would be compared with a similar group of elementary school children in order to answer the research question.

There are ethical considerations in studying children that some other disciplines may not face. Children should never be manipulated or put in danger in designing an experiment to answer research questions. Similarly, experiments that would not be in a child's best interests should not be conducted. Studies of abuse and neglect, for example, rely on retrospective techniques in which children who have already been abused report what has previously happened to them. No ethical researcher would ever put children at risk in order to observe the effects of abuse on children. Because of these ethical constraints, it can be frustrating for a researcher to fully answer questions raised in a research project. Additionally, it may take years to demonstrate the effectiveness of intervention for a particular social problem. Consequently, research on children and resultant intervention initiatives rarely offer "quick fixes" to the problems of children and society.

Future Directions

The study of children in society can begin to offer solutions to many of the more pressing societal problems. Quality childcare, parenting skills, education, stress reduction, affordable housing, job training, and humane political policies are a few ideas for solutions to some of the controversies that will be raised in this book.

The imbalance between work and family in the United States has created problems in the economy as well as in the family system. Workers are expected to produce quality goods and services, but they receive little social support in raising their families. Employers must acknowledge the strain that workers feel as they are pulled between work and family responsibilities. Health insurance, family-friendly work policies, flexible work schedules, parental and dependent care leave, exercise facilities, quality childcare and sick childcare, on-site or nearby one-stop service centers with post offices, grocery stores, and dry cleaners would be ways of providing support for families in the workplace.

Schools contribute to the problems of childcare arrangements by keeping to an antiquated schedule that was first developed to meet the needs of the farm family. Years ago, schools were let out in the early afternoon and all summer so that children could help with the crops, livestock, and other farm-related chores before sunset. However, ours has been a predominantly industrial society for a large part of the twentieth century and into the twenty-first century. As a result, a different type of schedule is required. Many concerned families advocate activities for children after school and schools that are open all year long to match the schedules of workers. The economy has changed and families have changed; why have educational institutions remained static?

The majority of children somehow manage to grow and develop successfully in a variety of family forms, but the stressors on all families are constantly increasing, which may, in turn, decrease the likelihood of continued success. Parents worry that the cost of a college education will be more than they can afford; parents worry about their children and AIDS, violence, and drugs; parents are concerned that in adulthood their children will not be able to live as well as they have lived. Families need emotional support, and parents need opportunities to learn stress management and parenting skills.

Society can promote the optimal growth and development of its children by taking responsibility for them. There is an old saying, "It takes a village to raise a child." Our society can raise its children by establishing policies in schools, workplaces, and other institutions that reflect the importance of nurturing children.

Unit 1

Infancy

*I*nfancy and toddlerhood encompass the time period from birth to age two or three. During this time, the most dramatic growth of a child's life takes place. Traditionally, much of the literature on infancy has dealt with the physical aspects of development; more recently, however, researchers, practitioners, and policy makers have begun to be concerned with the interaction of brain development on later learning and the social and emotional aspects of the infant's development.

The issues examined in this section focus on how the family and social institutions influence children's development from the time they are born.

Selected, Edited, and with Issue Framing Material by:
Kourtney T. Vaillancourt, *New Mexico State University*

ISSUE

Does Maternal Employment Have Negative Effects on Children's Development?

YES: Patricia M. Anderson, Kristin F. Butcher, and Phillip B. Levine, from "Maternal Employment and Overweight Children," *National Bureau of Economic Research* (2002)

NO: Daniel de Vise, from "Study: Working Mothers Not Necessarily Harmful to Child Development," *The Washington Post* (2010)

Learning Outcomes

After reading this issue, you should be able to:

- Summarize the effects that maternal employment can have on children.
- Discuss differences in outcomes based on when mothers return to work.
- Explain why some researchers believe there is a link between maternal employment and delinquency.

ISSUE SUMMARY

YES: Researchers Patricia Anderson, Kristin Butcher, and Phillip Levine from the National Bureau of Economic Research conclude that there is a connection between maternal employment and the risk of children being overweight.

NO: Daniel de Vise describes the results of a study conducted at Columbia University, which indicate that the negative and positive effects of maternal employment balance each other out to yield a neutral effect.

The number of women who combine work and motherhood has risen steadily in the past 35 years or so. Fifty-six percent of married mothers with a child under age 1 are employed, and 59 percent of unmarried mothers with a child under 1 are employed. The percentages of women entering the labor force increases as their children get older. Sixty-two percent of married mothers with a child aged 2 are working, and 75 percent of unmarried moms with a child aged 2 are working. Attitudes toward maternal employment have changed somewhat because of societal changes. It has become more socially acceptable today for moms to work. As more women obtain high-profile jobs in politics and corporations, more workplace assistance programs have been developed. These include on-site child care, flexible work hours, and allowing moms to work from home via computer technology. The realization

that it is an economic necessity for single moms as well as both parents in a dual-parent household to work has created more of an acceptance for working mothers. Many families need two incomes to make ends meet.

Time-saving appliances such as self-cleaning ovens, dishwashers, and microwave ovens have given working moms more time to spend with their children. Obtaining food for dinner from the growing number of restaurants offering drive-through or pick-up service has also relieved working moms from the hassle of running home from work to make dinner.

Of course, these time-saving means are only available to those who can afford them. Women with lower wages still struggle to balance work and family time. Welfare reform created a predicament for those who believed mothers should stay at home with their infants. With no governmental monetary support, how does a single mom stay at home with her children and still make a living for her family?

As more women moved into the workforce in the 1960s, research on maternal employment's effects on children became a popular topic of study. For the past 20 years, maternal employment has evolved from being studied as a single factor affecting children's development to being studied as a more complex issue. It was once thought that maternal employment had a direct single influence on children. Now researchers agree that maternal employment is more than a question of whether or not the mother works. The issue needs to be studied within the context of the family, the society, and cultural norms. Researchers do agree that maternal employment's effects on children need to be examined through the interaction of multiple variables, such as child-care quality, control over work situation, and family and societal support systems. They do not, however, agree on which sets of variables combine to give an accurate picture of how a mother's employment affects children's development. Study on maternal employment's effects must face the complicated task of simultaneously answering these questions. What quality of child care does the child receive? How does the mother feel about working? What societal and family support do the mother and child receive?

Researchers are not only divided on what variables to study, there is also a lack of agreement about what methods to use in studying maternal employment effects. For example, some researchers combine several social classes to study the interactive effects of working mothers with child-care arrangements, whereas others examine only one social class and how it intersects with the mother's personality traits and type of work and family environment. It is difficult to control for all characteristics that may affect the outcome of studies on maternal employment. Researchers suggest that more studies be conducted on a larger population so that they might generalize the results for the population as a whole. It is also suggested that the research methods include a larger diversity of ethnic groups and social classes to gain a better understanding of how maternal employment affects a child's development and behavioral outcomes.

The effects of maternal employment on children are determined by many factors such as mother's work satisfaction and morale, amount of and control over work, and mother's perception of quality versus quantity time with her children. Depending on which studies one reads, how the data were collected, and which combination of variables was studied, different conclusions are reported. For example, some studies show that working moms spend more quality time with their children than nonworking moms, while other studies show exactly the opposite results.

Research on maternal employment continues to become more refined, yet the question still remains: Should moms stay home with their babies? Often women who have the opportunity to do so will drop out of the workforce for at least the first few years to stay home and care for their children in order to make a connection. The concept that mother-child attachment in the first few years is critical to the child's later development has been established from years of significant research. Conversely, other research suggests that quality child-care providers may be able to meet the same attachment needs that mothers previously met. In addition, research shows that being exposed to a variety of quality caregivers, including other family members, fosters positive personality characteristics and independence in the child later on.

Young children want to be with their parents and need their parents to care for them. In an ideal world, most people want babies to be cared for by someone who loves them. In all but extreme abuse cases, this is generally the mom or dad. In our society, those who want to stay at home and care for their children should have the opportunity to do so. Yet, the economic environment prevents this from happening. Perhaps another way to look at the issue of maternal employment's effects on children's development is to develop ways to allow moms who want to stay home to raise their children to do so and to give social support to those moms who want to work outside the home.

In the YES selection, Patricia Anderson, Kristin Butcher, and Phillip Leving argue that maternal employment has negative effects on children, in that it increases the likelihood for overweight children. They describe how these effects are probably caused by time constraints that working mothers have, which limit their ability to supervise a child's nutritional intake and energy expenditure. In the NO selection, Daniel de Vise describes a study that indicates that maternal employment does not affect children's development negatively or positively. He found that maternal employment during the child's first year of life has negative and positive effects that balance each other out.

YES ↵

Patricia M. Anderson, Kristin F. Butcher, and Phillip B. Levine

Maternal Employment and Overweight Children

The increase in maternal employment and the rise in overweight children represent two of the most notable trends in the American family over the past several decades. From 1970 to 1999, the fraction of married women with children under six who participate in the labor force doubled, rising from 30 percent to 62 percent. Married women with children ages 6 to 17 dramatically increased their labor force participation as well, rising from 49 percent to 77 percent over this period (U.S. Bureau of the Census, 2000). The prevalence of overweight children has also soared. Over the 1963–1970 period 4 percent of children between the ages of 6 and 11 were defined to be overweight; that level had more than tripled by 1999, reaching 13 percent (Centers for Disease Control, 2001). Childhood overweight may be one of the most significant health issue facing children today. Thus, a better understanding of its determinants is of critical importance.

The existence of upward trends in both maternal employment and overweight among children could simply be a coincidence. In fact, the prevalence of overweight and obesity in adults has increased as well. However, the incidence of overweight in children relative to adults has increased. In the 1960's the ratio of overweight among children to adults was about 0.3, but had risen to almost 0.5 by 1999 (Centers for Disease Control, 2001). The purpose of this paper is to explore whether the relationship between maternal employment and childhood overweight is causal.

Using the National Longitudinal Survey of Youth (NLSY), supplemented with additional information from the 1988–1994 National Health and Nutrition Examination Survey (NHANES III) and the 1994–1996, 1998 Continuing Survey of Food Intakes by Individuals (CSFII), we first document the extent to which a raw correlation exists between maternal employment and overweight. The remainder of the paper attempts to identify whether these simple relationships are causal, or whether they reflect a spurious correlation in which children whose mothers work fulltime would still be overweight even if their mothers did not work. Our results indicate that those mothers who worked more intensively, in the form of greater hours per week, since their child's birth are indeed significantly more likely to have an overweight child. A mother who worked an additional 10 hours per week is estimated to increase the likelihood of her child being overweight by roughly one-half to one full percentage point. This effect is too small to explain a large fraction of the time series trend in childhood obesity, however, indicating that other factors must have played a larger role. . . .

Discussion

Overall, the results of this analysis indicate that a positive relationship exists between maternal employment and childhood overweight. In particular, we have found that a measure of the intensity of mother's work over the child's lifetime is consistently shown to be positively related to the child's likelihood of being overweight. A 10-hour increase in the average hours worked per week while working over the child's entire life is estimated to increase the likelihood that the child is overweight by about one half to one full percentage point. Thus, a mother moving from part-time (20 hours per week) work to full-time (40 hours) work is expected to increase the probability that her child is overweight by 1 to 2 percentage points. On the other hand, we found no evidence that the number of weeks a mother works over her child's life has any impact on the likelihood that her child will be overweight. These findings suggest that the link between maternal employment and a child's weight status may be the time constraints faced by mothers who work intensively. This result makes sense if it is the day-to-day routines that matter for a mother's ability to supervise her child's nutritional intake and energy expenditure. Working fewer hours per week allows more time for shopping, cooking, and energy expending play dates or organized sports. . . .

One of the other potentially important factors is the growth of adult overweight and obesity. Estimates indicate that obesity (BMI greater than 30) among women between the ages of 30 and 39 rose from 15 to 26 percent between 1976–80 and 1988–94 and overweight (BMI greater than 25) rose from 35 to 47 percent over this period. To the extent that adult behavior changes nutritional patterns in households in a way that affects children increased overweight among adults should correlate with increased overweight among children. Based on the estimates (and with all appropriate precautions against a causal interpretation of those findings), these increases in adult BMI would be predicted to increase childhood overweight by 0.9 percentage points. Therefore the increase in adult weight problems can "explain" about 11 percent in the trend in overweight among children. This effect is only slightly bigger than the effect of increases in the intensity of mothers' work habits. Nevertheless, even combining these two potential contributors leaves most of the trend in childhood overweight unexplained.

This project lays the groundwork for future research into the causes of childhood overweight. The contribution of this work is several-fold. First, much of the research on childhood overweight reports simple correlations between overweight and various characteristics of the child or the family. This project is among the first to grapple with issues of causality. It presents robust evidence of a positive and significant impact of maternal work on the probability that a child is overweight. Further, it presents prima facie evidence that the mechanism through which this takes place is constraints on mother's time; it is hours per week, not the number of weeks worked, that affects children's probability of overweight.

There is much more to learn about causal factors related to the epidemic of overweight among children in the United States. These include understanding direct contributors to childhood overweight and the mechanisms through which mothers' working translates into overweight children. For example, how does child care quality affect children's nutrition and energy expenditure? Additionally, we need to know more about children's opportunities for vigorous exercise, including physical education in school, after-school programs, and access to parks or other recreational facilities. This deeper understanding is important if society is going to develop appropriate policy responses to this important public health issue.

Patricia M. Anderson is Professor of Economics at Dartmouth and a Research Associate at the National Bureau of Economic Research in Cambridge, MA. She received her BA Economics and Mathematics from William and Mary in 1985, and her PhD in Economics from Princeton in 1991. Prof. Anderson's research interests fall broadly in the field of applied microeconomics, with specific interests in child health & nutrition and in social insurance programs. She is a Co-editor for the Journal of Human Resources and is on the Editorial Board for B.E. Journals in Economic Analysis and Policy.

Kristin F. Butcher is Assistant Professor of Economics, Boston College (on leave), and a Program Officer at the MacArthur Foundation.

Phillip B. Levine is Katharine Coman and A. Barton Hepburn Professor of Economics and the Economics Department Chair at Wellesley College.

Levine's Research has examined such issues as the impact of abortion policy changes on pregnancy, abortion, and birth; the impact of the business cycle on retirement behavior; and the ability of alternative public policies to raise the adult incomes of children who grow up in poverty.

Daniel de Vise   ➡ **NO**

Study: Working Mothers Not Necessarily Harmful to Child Development

A new study finds that babies raised by working mothers don't necessarily suffer cognitive setbacks, an encouraging finding that follows a raft of previous reports suggesting that women with infants were wiser to stay home.

Researchers at Columbia University say they are among the first to measure the full effect of maternal employment on child development—not just the potential harm caused by a mother's absence from the home, but the prospective benefits that come with her job, including higher family income and better child care.

In a 113-page monograph, released this week, the authors conclude "that the overall effect of 1st-year maternal employment on child development is neutral."

The report is based on data from the most comprehensive child-care study to date, the National Institute of Child Health and Human Development Study of Early Child Care. It followed more than 1,000 children from 10 geographic areas through first grade, tracking their development and family characteristics.

Infants raised by mothers with full-time jobs scored somewhat lower on cognitive tests, deficits that persisted into first grade. But that negative effect was offset by several positives. Working mothers had higher income. They were more likely to seek high-quality child care. And they displayed greater "maternal sensitivity," or responsiveness toward their children, than stay-at-home mothers. Those positives canceled out the negatives.

The study may bring hope to working mothers, who have labored under a collective societal guilt since the 2002 publication of landmark research showing that early maternal employment hampered child development. The same research team behind that report produced this one.

"We can say now, from this study, what we couldn't say before: There's a slight risk, and here's the three things that you, Mom, can do to make a difference," said Jeanne Brooks-Gunn, the lead author. "This particular research has a positive message for mothers that the earlier research didn't."

The study, "First-Year Maternal Employment and Child Development in the First 7 Years," reaffirms the now-established point that women who work full time in the first year of motherhood risk mild developmental harm to their children. Part-time employment has no negative effect, nor does it matter whether a mother works full time after the first year.

The reason may be that a mother with a full-time job cannot provide an infant "the kinds of intensive interaction that babies require," needs that diminish in the toddler years, Brooks-Gunn said. High-quality child care, too, is hard to find for an infant.

The new study is "every bit as important as you might think," because it suggests mothers can decide, without guilt, "whether they want to stay home with their children," said Greg Duncan, a scholar at the University of California at Irvine, who is president of the Society for Research in Child Development.

DANIEL DE VISE is higher education reporter at *The Washington Post* and author of the College Inc. blog. He has worked as a journalist for 20 years, including stints at the Boca Raton News, Long Beach Press-Telegram, San Diego Union Tribune, and Miami Herald.

EXPLORING THE ISSUE

Does Maternal Employment Have Negative Effects on Children's Development?

Critical Thinking and Reflection

1. de Vise talks about how the study he describes identifies the guilt that working mothers may face. In your opinion, what is society's role in that guilt?
2. What are some creative ways that you can identify that would allow moms who want to stay home to raise their children to do so, as well as to give social support to those moms who want to work outside the home?
3. What do you consider to be the biggest influence on mothers' decision making about whether or not they should work outside of the home?

Is There Common Ground?

Each reading in this issue centers around a research group at Columbia University. Some of the information is hopeful, and some of it is bothersome. Yet, the researchers all recognize that many mothers must work and therefore must work to mitigate any potential negative effects that their working may have on their children.

Families must have discussions about the type of care that they want for their children, and how they can accommodate their lifestyles to obtain that care. And, society must take action to support mothers in whatever choice they make by providing quality child care for those who work and supportive leave policies and social support systems for those who do not.

Additional Resources

Columbia University School of Social Work. (2010). New Evidence on First-Year Maternal Employment and Child Outcomes. Retrieved on March 8, 2011, from www.columbia.edu/cu/ssw/news/jul10/maternity.html

An article posted on the Internet that provides a more nuanced understanding of how maternal employment might impact children.

Parenthood in America. (1998). The Effects of the Mother's Employment on the Family and the Child. Retrieved on March 8, 2011, from http://parenthood.library.wisc.edu/Hoffman/Hoffman.html#top

An article posted on the Internet that provides information on maternal employment trends throughout the years and discusses multiple factors that impact the effects of maternal employment on children.

Internet References . . .

Working Mother

www.workingmother.com/

USA Today (Society for the Advancement of Education)—Positive Effects of Working Mothers (2011). Retrieved on March 8, 2011

An article posted on the Internet that discusses some positive effects that have been identified for mothers who work.

http://findarticles.com/p/articles/mi_m1272/is_2659_128/ai_61586736/

Selected, Edited, and with Issue Framing Material by:
Kourtney T. Vaillancourt, *New Mexico State University*

ISSUE

Should Parents Be Allowed to Genetically Engineer Their Children?

YES: Antonio Regalado, from "Engineering the Perfect Baby," *MIT Technology* (2015)

NO: Akshat Rathi, from "The Pros and Cons of Genetically Engineering Your Children," *Quartz* (2015)

Learning Outcomes

After reading this issue, you will be able to:

- List some of the reasons that children might be genetically engineered.
- Identify some of the ethical issues that are related to genetic engineering.
- List some of the reasons that are given by advocates to support the use of genetic engineering.
- Summarize the vision of genetic engineers.

ISSUE SUMMARY

YES: Antonio Regalado urges caution in, but does advocate for, moving forward with genetically engineering children, discussing some of the existing ethical and moral concerns that scientists have identified.

NO: Akshat Rathi reports on the conclusions of a meeting of minds regarding the practice of genetic engineering. Their conclusion is that we neither know enough about safety issues or how humans will respond to such practices to condone them.

With advances in genetic research, including being able to identify which genes contribute to characteristics such as aggression and intelligence, society's debate over the possibility of replicating more favorable attitudes in unborn children is becoming even more heated.

On the one hand, if we were able to identify genes that might cause someone to develop an incurable disease and shut them off, the potential to save lives is pretty appealing. And, if we are able to determine the personality and attributes of children when they are being created, we might be able to realize a more perfect society. On the other hand, the potential for the science to still have kinks that have not been worked out is pretty big. And, there are those who argue that "creating" babies in a laboratory goes against nature.

So, is genetically engineering children morally and ethically wrong? Is the potential benefit to families and society wroth the risks that come along? Could our society ever truly get to a point of utopia where there is peace because everyone's "violent" genes have been turned off?

As you read the following selections, try to suspend the personal attitudes about this issue that you may have developed. Try to learn about the process, what it truly is intended to do, and what it could possibly accomplish. In addition, consider what could be the consequences of allowing this. Some questions to consider include the following: Would we be better off if the federal government decided to fund genetic engineering research to help regulate it? Would we be better off if this was banned completely and totally?

In the following selections, Antonio Regalado discusses some of the existing ethical and moral concerns that scientists have identified for genetic engineering of children. He does urge caution in how we move forward but finds it desirable to continue to work on this task. Akshat Rathi provides a report about a meeting of professionals who have concluded that we do not yet have enough information or knowledge about the safety issues related to genetic engineering to advocate for it moving forward.

YES ↵

Antonio Regalado

Engineering the Perfect Baby

Scientists Are Developing Ways to Edit the DNA of Tomorrow's Children. Should They Stop Before It's Too Late?

If anyone had devised a way to create a genetically engineered baby, I figured George Church would know about it.

At his labyrinthine laboratory on the Harvard Medical School campus, you can find researchers giving *E. Coli* a novel genetic code never seen in nature. Around another bend, others are carrying out a plan to use DNA engineering to resurrect the woolly mammoth. His lab, Church likes to say, is the center of a new technological genesis—one in which man rebuilds creation to suit himself. When I visited the laboratory last June, Church proposed that I speak to a young postdoctoral scientist named Luhan Yang. A Harvard recruit from Beijing, she'd been a key player in developing a powerful new technology for editing DNA, called CRISPR-Cas9. With Church, Yang had founded a small biotechnology company to engineer the genomes of pigs and cattle, sliding in beneficial genes and editing away bad ones.

As I listened to Yang, I waited for a chance to ask my real questions: Can any of this be done to human beings? Can we improve the human gene pool? The position of much of mainstream science has been that such meddling would be unsafe, irresponsible, and even impossible. But Yang didn't hesitate. Yes, of course, she said. In fact, the Harvard laboratory had a project under way to determine how it could be achieved. She flipped open her laptop to a PowerPoint slide titled "Germline Editing Meeting."

Here it was: a technical proposal to alter human heredity. "Germ line" is biologists' jargon for the egg and sperm, which combine to form an embryo. By editing the DNA of these cells or the embryo itself, it could be possible to correct disease genes and pass those genetic fixes on to future generations. Such a technology could be used to rid families of scourges like cystic fibrosis. It might also be possible to install genes that offer lifelong protection against infection, Alzheimer's, and, Yang told me, maybe the effects of aging. Such history-making medical advances could be as important to this century as vaccines were to the last.

That's the promise. The fear is that germ-line engineering is a path toward a dystopia of superpeople and designer babies for those who can afford it. Want a child with blue eyes and blond hair? Why not design a highly intelligent group of people who could be tomorrow's leaders and scientists?

Just three years after its initial development, CRISPR technology is already widely used by biologists as a kind of search-and-replace tool to alter DNA, even down to the level of a single letter. It's so precise that it's expected to turn into a promising new approach for gene therapy in people with devastating illnesses. The idea is that physicians could directly correct a faulty gene, say, in the blood cells of a patient with sickle cell anemia (see "Genome Surgery"). But that kind of gene therapy wouldn't affect germ cells, and the changes in the DNA wouldn't get passed to future generations.

In contrast, the genetic changes created by germ-line engineering would be passed on, and that's what has made the idea seem so objectionable. So far, caution and ethical concerns have had the upper hand. A dozen countries, not including the United States, have banned germ-line engineering, and scientific societies have unanimously concluded that it would be too risky to do. The European Union's convention on human rights and biomedicine says tampering with the gene pool would be a crime against "human dignity" and human rights. But all these declarations were made before it was actually feasible to precisely engineer the germ line. Now, with CRISPR, it is possible.

The experiment Yang described, though not simple, would go like this: The researchers hoped to obtain, from a hospital in New York, the ovaries of a woman undergoing surgery for ovarian cancer caused by a mutation in a gene called *BRCA1*. Working with another Harvard laboratory, that of antiaging specialist David Sinclair, they would extract immature egg cells that could be coaxed to grow and divide in the laboratory. Yang would use CRISPR in these cells to correct the DNA of the *BRCA1* gene. They would try to create a viable egg without the genetic error that caused the woman's cancer.

Yang would later tell me that she dropped out of the project not long after we spoke. Yet it remained difficult to know if the experiment she described was occurring, canceled, or awaiting publication. Sinclair said that a collaboration between the two labs was ongoing, but then, like several other scientists whom I'd asked about germline engineering, he stopped replying to my e-mails.

Regardless of the fate of that particular experiment, human germ-line engineering has become a burgeoning research concept. At least three other centers in the United States are working on it, as are scientists in China, in the United Kingdom, and at a biotechnology company called OvaScience, based in Cambridge, MA, that boasts some of the world's leading fertility doctors on its advisory board.

All this means that germ-line engineering is much further along than anyone imagined.

The objective of these groups is to demonstrate that it's possible to produce children free of specific genes involved in inherited disease. If it's possible to correct the DNA in a woman's egg, or a man's sperm, those cells could be used in an in vitro fertilization (IVF) clinic to produce an embryo and then a child. It might also be possible to directly edit the DNA of an early-stage IVF embryo using CRISPR. Several people interviewed by *MIT Technology Review* said that such experiments had already been carried out in China and that results describing edited embryos were pending publication. These people, including two high-ranking specialists, didn't wish to comment publicly because the papers are under review.

All this means that germ-line engineering is much further along than anyone imagined. "What you are talking about is a major issue for all humanity," says Merle Berger, one of the founders of Boston IVF, a network of fertility clinics that is among the largest in the world and helps more than a thousand women get pregnant each year. "It would be the biggest thing that ever happened in our field." Berger predicts that repairing genes involved in serious inherited diseases will win wide public acceptance but says the idea of using the technology beyond that would cause a public uproar because "everyone would want the perfect child": people might pick and choose eye color and eventually intelligence. "These are things we

talk about all the time," he says. "But we have never had the opportunity to do it."

Editing Embryos

How easy would it be to edit a human embryo using CRISPR? Very easy, experts say. "Any scientist with molecular biology skills and knowledge of how to work with [embryos] is going to be able to do this," says Jennifer Doudna, a biologist at the University of California, Berkeley, who in 2012 codiscovered how to use CRISPR to edit genes.

To find out how it could be done, I visited the laboratory of Guoping Feng, a biologist at MIT's McGovern Institute for Brain Research, where a colony of marmoset monkeys is being established with the aim of using CRISPR to create accurate models of human brain diseases. To create the models, Feng will edit the DNA of embryos and then transfer them into female marmosets to produce live monkeys. One gene Feng hopes to alter in the animals is *SHANK3*. The gene is involved in how neurons communicate; when it's damaged in children, it is known to cause autism.

Feng said that before CRISPR, it was not possible to introduce precise changes into a primate's DNA. With CRISPR, the technique should be relatively straightforward. The CRISPR system includes a gene-snipping enzyme and a guide molecule that can be programmed to target unique combinations of the DNA letters, A, G, C, and T; get these

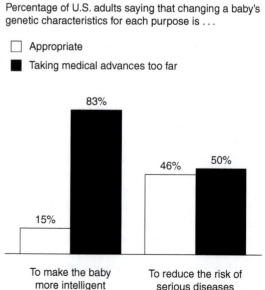

Genetic Modification of Babies

Percentage of U.S. adults saying that changing a baby's genetic characteristics for each purpose is . . .

☐ Appropriate

■ Taking medical advances too far

83%

46%   50%

15%

To make the baby more intelligent

To reduce the risk of serious diseases

ingredients into a cell and they will cut and modify the genome at the targeted sites.

But CRISPR is not perfect—and it would be a very haphazard way to edit human embryos, as Feng's efforts to create gene-edited marmosets show. To employ the CRISPR system in the monkeys, his students simply inject the chemicals into a fertilized egg, which is known as a zygote—the stage just before it starts dividing.

Feng said the efficiency with which CRISPR can delete or disable a gene in a zygote is about 40 percent, whereas making specific edits, or swapping DNA letters, works less frequently—more like 20 percent of the time. Like a person, a monkey has two copies of most genes, one from each parent. Sometimes both copies get edited, but sometimes just one does, or neither. Only about half the embryos will lead to live births, and of those that do, many could contain a mixture of cells with edited DNA and without. If you add up the odds, you find you'd need to edit 20 embryos to get a live monkey with the version you want.

That's not an insurmountable problem for Feng, since the MIT breeding colony will give him access to many monkey eggs, and he'll be able to generate many embryos. However, it would present obvious problems in humans. Putting the ingredients of CRISPR into a human embryo would be scientifically trivial. But it wouldn't be practical for much just yet. This is one reason that many scientists view such an experiment (whether or not it has really occurred in China) with scorn, seeing it more as a provocative bid to grab attention than as real science. Rudolf Jaenisch, an MIT biologist who works across the street from Feng and who in the 1970s created the first gene-modified mice, calls attempts to edit human embryos "totally premature." He says he hopes these papers will be rejected and not published. "It's just a sensational thing that will stir things up," says Jaenisch. "We know it's possible, but is it of practical use? I kind of doubt it."

For his part, Feng told me he approves of the idea of germ-line engineering. Isn't the goal of medicine to reduce suffering? Considering the state of the technology, however, he thinks actual gene-edited humans are "10 to 20 years away." Among other problems, CRISPR can introduce off-target effects or change bits of the genome far from where scientists had intended. Any human embryo altered with CRISPR today would carry the risk that its genome had been changed in unexpected ways. But, Feng said, such problems may eventually be ironed out, and edited people will be born. "To me, it's possible in the long run to dramatically improve health, lower costs. It's a kind of prevention," he said. "It's hard to predict the future, but correcting disease risks is definitely a possibility and should be supported. I think it will be a reality."

Editing Eggs

Elsewhere in the Boston area, scientists are exploring a different approach to engineering the germ line, one that is technically more demanding but probably more powerful. This strategy combines CRISPR with unfolding discoveries related to stem cells. Scientists at several centers, including Church's, think they will soon be able to use stem cells to produce eggs and sperm in the laboratory. Unlike embryos, stem cells can be grown and multiplied. Thus, they could offer a vastly improved way to create edited offspring with CRISPR. The recipe goes like this: First, edit the genes of the stem cells. Second, turn them into an egg or sperm. Third, produce an offspring.

Some investors got an early view of the technique on December 17, at the Benjamin Hotel in Manhattan, during commercial presentations by OvaScience. The company, which was founded four years ago, aims to commercialize the scientific work of David Sinclair, who is based at Harvard, and Jonathan Tilly, an expert on egg stem cells and the chairman of the biology department at Northeastern University (see "10 Emerging Technologies: Egg Stem Cells," May/June 2012). It made the presentations as part of a successful effort to raise $132 million in new capital during January.

During the meeting, Sinclair, a velvet-voiced Australian whom *Time* last year named one of the "100 Most Influential People in the World," took the podium and provided Wall Street with a peek at what he called "truly world-changing" developments. People would look back at this moment in time and recognize it as a new chapter in "how humans control their bodies," he said, because it would let parents determine "when and how they have children and how healthy those children are actually going to be."

The company has not perfected its stem cell technology—it has not reported that the eggs it grows in the laboratory are viable—but Sinclair predicted that functional eggs were "a when, and not an if." Once the technology works, he said, infertile women will be able to produce hundreds of eggs, and maybe hundreds of embryos. Using DNA sequencing to analyze their genes, they could pick among them for the healthiest ones.

Genetically improved children may also be possible. Sinclair told the investors that he was trying to alter the DNA of these egg stem cells using gene editing work, he later told me he was doing with Church's lab. "We think the new technologies with genome editing will allow it to be used on individuals who aren't just interested in using IVF to have children but have healthier children as well, if there is a genetic disease in their family," Sinclair told the investors. He gave the example of Huntington's disease, caused by a gene that will trigger a fatal brain condition even in someone who inherits only one copy. Sinclair said gene editing could be used to remove the lethal gene defect from an egg cell. His goal, and that of OvaScience, is to "correct those mutations before we generate your child," he said. "It's still experimental, but there is no reason to expect it won't be possible in coming years."

Sinclair spoke to me briefly on the phone while he was navigating in a cab across a snowed-in Boston, but later he referred my questions to OvaScience. When I contacted OvaScience, Cara Mayfield, a spokeswoman, said its executives could not comment because of their travel schedules but confirmed that the company was working on treating inherited disorders with gene editing. What was surprising to me was that OvaScience's research in "crossing the germ line," as critics of human engineering sometimes put it, has generated scarcely any notice. In December 2013, OvaScience even announced it was putting $1.5 million into a joint venture with a synthetic biology company called Intrexon, whose R&D objectives include gene-editing eggs to "prevent the propagation" of human disease "in future generations."

When I reached Tilly at Northeastern, he laughed when I told him what I was calling about. "It's going to be a hot-button issue," he said. Tilly also said his laboratory was trying to edit egg stem cells with CRISPR "right now" to rid them of an inherited genetic disease that he didn't want to name. Tilly emphasized that there are "two pieces of the puzzle"—one being stem cells and the other gene editing. The ability to create large numbers of egg stem cells is critical, because only with sizable quantities can genetic changes be stably introduced using CRISPR, characterized using DNA sequencing, and carefully studied to check for mistakes before producing an egg.

Tilly predicted that the whole end-to-end technology—cells to stem cells, stem cells to sperm or egg and then to offspring—would end up being worked out first in animals, such as cattle, either by his laboratory or by companies such as eGenesis, the spin-off from the Church laboratory working on livestock. But he isn't sure what the next step should be with edited human eggs. You wouldn't want to fertilize one "willy nilly," he said. You'd be making a potential human being.

And doing that would raise questions he's not sure he can answer. He told me, "'Can you do it?' is one thing. If you can, then the most important questions come up. 'Would you do it? Why would you want to do it? What is the purpose?' As scientists we want to know if it's feasible, but then we get into the bigger questions, and it's not a science question—it's a society question."

Improving Humans

If germ-line engineering becomes part of medical practice, it could lead to transformative changes in human well-being, with consequences to people's life span, identity, and economic output. But it would create ethical dilemmas and social challenges. What if these improvements were available only to the richest societies, or the richest people? An in vitro fertility procedure costs about $20,000 in the United States. Add genetic testing and egg donation or a surrogate mother, and the price soars toward $100,000.

Others believe the idea is dubious because it's not medically necessary. Hank Greely, a lawyer and ethicist at Stanford University, says proponents "can't really say what it is good for." The problem, says Greely, is that it's already possible to test the DNA of IVF embryos and pick healthy ones, a process that adds about $4,000 to the cost of a fertility procedure. A man with Huntington's, for instance, could have his sperm used to fertilize a dozen of his partner's eggs. Half those embryos would not have the Huntington's gene, and those could be used to begin a pregnancy.

Indeed, some people are adamant that germ-line engineering is being pushed ahead with "false arguments." That is the view of Edward Lanphier, CEO of Sangamo Biosciences, a California biotechnology company that is using another gene-editing technique, called zinc fingers nucleases, to try to treat HIV in adults by altering their blood cells. "We've looked at [germ-line engineering] for a disease rationale, and there is none," he says. "You can do it. But there really isn't a medical reason. People say, well, we don't want children born with this, or born with that—but it's a completely false argument and a slippery slope toward much more unacceptable uses."

Critics cite a host of fears. Children would be the subject of experiments. Parents would be influenced by genetic advertising from IVF clinics. Germ-line engineering would encourage the spread of allegedly superior traits. And it would affect people not yet born, without their being able to agree to it. The American Medical Association, for instance, holds that germ-line engineering shouldn't be done "at this time" because it "affects the welfare of future generations" and could cause "unpredictable and irreversible results." But like a lot of official statements that forbid changing the genome, the AMA's, which was last updated in 1996, predates today's technology. "A lot of people just agreed to these statements," says Greely. "It wasn't hard to renounce something that you couldn't do."

The fear? A dystopia of superpeople and designer babies for those who can afford it.

Others predict that hard-to-oppose medical uses will be identified. A couple with several genetic diseases at once might not be able to find a suitable embryo. Treating infertility is another possibility. Some men don't produce any sperm, a condition called azoospermia. One cause is a genetic defect in which a region of about one million to six million DNA letters is missing from the Y chromosome. It might be possible to take a skin cell from such a man, turn it into a stem cell, repair the DNA, and then make sperm, says Werner Neuhausser, a young Austrian doctor who splits his time between the Boston IVF fertility-clinic network and Harvard's Stem Cell Institute. "That will change medicine forever, right? You could cure infertility, that is for sure," he says.

I spoke with Church several times by telephone over the last few months, and he told me what's driving everything is the "incredible specificity" of CRISPR. Although not all the details have been worked out, he thinks the technology could replace DNA letters essentially without side effects. He says this is what makes it "tempting to use." Church says his laboratory is focused mostly on experiments in engineering animals. He added that his laboratory would not make or edit human embryos, calling such a step "not our style."

What is Church's style is human enhancement. And he's been making a broad case that CRISPR can do more than eliminate disease genes. It can lead to augmentation. At meetings, some involving groups of "transhumanists" interested in next steps for human evolution, Church likes to show a slide on which he lists naturally occurring variants of around 10 genes that, when people are born with them, confer extraordinary qualities or resistance to disease. One makes your bones so hard they'll break a surgical drill. Another drastically cuts the risk of heart attacks. And a variant of the gene for the amyloid precursor protein, or APP, was found by Icelandic researchers to protect against Alzheimer's. People with it never get dementia and remain sharp into old age.

Church thinks CRISPR could be used to provide people with favorable versions of genes, making DNA edits that would act as vaccines against some of the most common diseases we face today. Although he told me anything "edgy" should be done only to adults who can consent, it's obvious to him that the earlier such interventions occur, the better.

Church tends to dodge questions about genetically modified babies. The idea of improving the human species has always had "enormously bad press," he wrote in the introduction to *Regenesis*, his 2012 book on synthetic biology, whose cover was a painting by Eustache Le Sueur of a bearded God creating the world. But that's ultimately what he's suggesting: enhancements in the form of protective genes. "An argument will be made that the ultimate prevention is that the earlier you go, the better the prevention," he told an audience at MIT's Media Lab last spring. "I do think it's the ultimate preventive, *if* we get to the point where it's very inexpensive, extremely safe, and very predictable." Church, who has a less cautious side, proceeded to tell the audience that he thought changing genes "is going to get to the point where it's like you are doing the equivalent of cosmetic surgery."

Some thinkers have concluded that we should not pass up the chance to make improvements to our species. "The human genome is not perfect," says John Harris, a bioethicist at Manchester University, in the United Kingdom. "It's ethically imperative to positively support this technology." By some measures, U.S. public opinion is not particularly negative toward the idea. A Pew Research survey carried out last August found that 46 percent of adults approved of genetic modification of babies to reduce the risk of serious diseases.

The same survey found that 83 percent said genetic modification to make a baby smarter would be "taking medical advances too far." But other observers say higher IQ is exactly what we should be considering. Nick Bostrom, an Oxford philosopher best known for his 2014 book *Superintelligence*, which raised alarms about the risks of artificial intelligence in computers, has also looked at whether humans could use reproductive technology to improve human intellect.

Although the ways in which genes affect intelligence aren't well understood and there are far too many relevant genes to permit easy engineering, such realities don't dim speculation on the possibility of high-tech eugenics.

"The human genome is not perfect. It's ethically imperative to positively support this technology."

What if everyone could be a little bit smarter? Or a few people could be a lot smarter? Even a small number of "super-enhanced" individuals, Bostrom wrote in a 2013 paper, could change the world through their creativity and discoveries, and through innovations that everyone else would use. In his view, genetic enhancement is an important long-range issue like climate change or financial planning by nations, "since human problem-solving ability is a factor in every challenge we face."

To some scientists, the explosive advance of genetics and biotech means germ-line engineering is inevitable. Of course, safety questions would be paramount. Before there's a genetically edited baby saying "Mama," there would have to be tests in rats, rabbits, and probably monkeys, to make sure they are normal. But ultimately, if the benefits seem to outweigh the risks, medicine would take the chance. "It was the same with IVF when it first happened," says Neuhausser. "We never really knew if that baby was going to be healthy at 40 or 50 years. But someone had to take the plunge."

Wine Country

In January, on Saturday the 24th, around 20 scientists, ethicists, and legal experts traveled to Napa Valley, California, for a retreat among the vineyards at the Carneros Inn. They had been convened by Doudna, the Berkeley scientist who codiscovered the CRISPR system a little over two years ago. She had become aware that scientists might be thinking of crossing the germ line, and she was concerned. Now she wanted to know: could they be stopped?

"We as scientists have come to appreciate that CRISPR is incredibly powerful. But that swings both ways. We need to make sure that it's applied carefully," Doudna told me. "The issue is especially human germ-line editing and the appreciation that this is now a capability in everyone's hands."

At the meeting, along with ethicists like Greely, was Paul Berg, a Stanford biochemist and Nobel Prize winner known for having organized the Asilomar Conference, a historic 1975 forum at which biologists reached an agreement on how to safely proceed with recombinant DNA, the newly discovered method of splicing DNA into bacteria.

Should there be an Asilomar for germ-line engineering? Doudna thinks so, but the prospects for consensus seem dim. Biotechnology research is now global, involving hundreds of thousands of people. There's no single authority that speaks for science, and no easy way to put the genie back in the bottle. Doudna told me she hoped that if American scientists agreed to a moratorium on human germ-line engineering, it might influence researchers elsewhere in the world to cease their work.

Doudna said she felt that a self-imposed pause should apply not only to making gene-edited babies but also to using CRISPR to alter human embryos, eggs, or sperm—as researchers at Harvard, Northeastern, and OvaScience are doing. "I don't feel that those experiments are appropriate to do right now in human cells that could turn into a person," she told me. "I feel that the research that needs to be done right now is to understand safety, efficacy, and delivery. And I think those experiments can be done in nonhuman systems. I would like to see a lot more work done before it's done for germ-line editing. I would favor a very cautious approach."

Not everyone agrees that germ-line engineering is such a big worry, or that experiments should be padlocked. Greely notes that in the United States, there are piles of regulations to keep laboratory science from morphing into a genetically modified baby anytime soon. "I would not want to use safety as an excuse for a non-safety-based ban," says Greely, who says he pushed back against talk of a moratorium. But he also says he agreed to sign Doudna's letter, which now reflects the consensus of the group. "Although I don't view this as a crisis moment, I think it's probably about time for us to have this discussion," he says.

(After this article was published online in March, Doudna's editorial appeared in *Science* [see "Scientists Call for a Summit on Gene-Edited Babies."] Along with Greely, Berg, and 15 others, she called for a global moratorium on any effort to use CRISPR to generate gene-edited children until researchers could determine "what clinical applications, if any, might in the future be deemed permissible." The group, however, endorsed basic research, including applying CRISPR to embryos. The final list of signatories included Church, although he did not attend the Napa meeting.)

As news has spread of germ-line experiments, some biotechnology companies now working on CRISPR have realized that they will have to take a stand. Nessan Bermingham is CEO of Intellia Therapeutics, a Boston startup that raised $15 million last year to develop CRISPR into gene therapy treatments for adults or children. He says germ-line engineering "is not on our commercial radar," and he suggests that his company could use its patents to prevent anyone from commercializing it.

"The technology is in its infancy," he says. "It is not appropriate for people to even be contemplating germ-line applications."

Bermingham told me he never imagined he'd have to be taking a position on genetically modified babies so soon. Modifying human heredity has always been a theoretical possibility. Suddenly it's a real one. But wasn't the point always to understand and control our own biology—to become masters over the processes that created us?

Doudna says she is also thinking about these issues. "It cuts to the core of who we are as people, and it makes you ask if humans should be exercising that kind of power," she told me. "There are moral and ethical issues, but one of the profound questions is just the appreciation that if germ-line editing is conducted in humans, that is changing human evolution." One reason she feels the research should slow down is to give scientists a chance to spend more time explaining what their next steps could be.

"Most of the public," she says, "does not appreciate what is coming."

This story was updated on April 23, 2015.

ANTONIO REGALADO is the senior editor for biomedicine for *MIT Technology Review*. He looks for stories about how technology is changing medicine and biomedical research. Before joining *MIT Technology Review* in July 2011, he lives in Sao Paulao, Brazil where he wrote about science, technology, and politics in Latin America for *Science* and other publications. From 2000 to 2009, he was the science reporter at the *Wall Street Journal* and later a foreign correspondent.

Akshat Rathi

 **NO**

The Pros and Cons of Genetically Engineering Your Children

From time to time, science troubles philosophers with difficult ethical questions. But none has been as difficult as considering permanently altering the genetic code of future generations. At a meeting that began on December 1 in Washington DC, the world's leading gene-editing experts met with ethicists, lawyers, and interested members of the public to decide whether it should be done.

Gene-editing tools have existed since 1975, when a meeting of a similar kind was held to discuss the future of genetic technology. But recent developments have made the technology safe enough to consider turning science fiction into reality. In fact, in April, Chinese researchers announced that they had conducted experiments to remove genes of an inheritable disease in human embryos (embryos that were alive but damaged, so they could not have become babies).

So the stakes are high. By eliminating "bad" genes from sperm and egg cells—called the "germ line"—these tools have the potential to permanently wipe out diseases caused by single mutations in genes, such as cystic fibrosis, Huntington's disease, or Tay-Sachs.

At the same time, there is huge uncertainty about what could go wrong if seemingly troubling genes are eliminated.

One of the key researchers in the field is Jennifer Doudna at the University of California, Berkeley. She has been touted for a Nobel Prize for the development of CRISPR-Cas9, a highly precise copy–paste genetic tool. In the build-up to the meeting, Doudna made her concerns clear in Nature:

"Human-germline editing for the purposes of creating genome-modified humans should not proceed at this time, partly because of the unknown social consequences, but also because the technology and our knowledge of the human genome are simply not ready to do so safely."

Her sentiments were echoed in a report released before the meeting by the Center for Genetics and Society. They believe that research in genetic tools must advance but only through therapy for adults (where genetic modifications are targeted at some cells in the body but not passed on to kids, such as in curing a form of inherited blindness). The report continues:

"But using the same techniques to modify embryos in order to make permanent, irreversible changes to future generations and to our common genetic heritage—the human germ line, as it is known—is far more problematic."

Consider sickle cell anemia, an occasionally fatal genetic disorder. Its genes, though clearly harmful, have persisted and spread because, while having two copies of the sickle cell gene causes anemia, having just one copy happens to provide protection against malaria, one of the most deadly diseases in human history. Had we not known about their benefits, eliminating sickle cell genes would have proved to be a bad idea.

More importantly, there is a worry that once you allow for designer babies you go down a slippery slope. Emily Smith Beitiks, disability researcher at the University of California, San Francisco, said recently:

"These proposed applications raise social justice questions and put us at risk of reviving eugenics—controlled breeding to increase the occurrence of 'desirable' heritable characteristics. Who gets to decide what diversity looks like and who is valued?"

But the history of science shows that it is hard to keep such a cat in the bag. Once developed, technologies have a way of finding their way into the hands of those who desire to use them. That worries George Church, a geneticist at Harvard Medical School, who has been a strong voice in this debate since the beginning. In Nature, he writes:

"Banning human-germlined editing could put a damper on the best medical research and instead drive the practice underground to black markets and uncontrolled medical tourism, which are fraught with much greater risk and misapplication."

And many believe that the risks of gene-editing are not that high anyway. Nathaniel Comfort, a historian of medicine at Johns Hopkins University in Baltimore, writes in Aeon:

"The dishes do not come à la carte. If you believe that made-to-order babies are possible, you oversimplify how genes work."

That is because abilities, such as intelligence, height, or personality traits, involve thousands of genes. So there may be some things that you cannot genetically enhance much, and certainly not safely. And even knowingly changing the human genome is not as big a deal as some make it out to be, Church notes:

"Offspring do not consent to their parents' intentional exposure to mutagenic sources that alter the germ line, including chemotherapy, high altitude, and alcohol— nor to decisions that reduce the prospects for future generations, such as misdirected economic investment and environmental mismanagement."

The meeting ended on December 3, and the committee of organizers—10 scientists and two bioethicists— came to a conclusion on the debate. They believe that the promises of germline editing are too great to scupper future developments. They endorse that research should continue in nonhuman embryos and "if, in the process of research, early human embryos . . . undergo gene editing, the modified cells should not be used to establish a pregnancy." That is because the committee believes that we neither know enough about safety issues to allow any clinical application nor enough about how society will respond to the use of this technology in humans.

And, yet, perhaps the last word on the debate should go to a woman in the audience at the meeting. Her child died only six days old after torturous seizures caused by a genetic ailment. She implored the research community, "If you have the skills and the knowledge to eliminate these diseases, then freakin' do it!"

Akshat Rathi is a reporter for Quartz in London. He has previously worked at The Economist and The Conversation. His writing has appeared in Nature, The Guardian, and The Hindu. He has a PhD in chemistry from Oxford University and a BTech in chemical engineering from the Institute of Chemical Technology, Mumbai.

EXPLORING THE ISSUE

Should Parents Be Allowed to Genetically Engineer Their Children?

Critical Thinking and Reflection

1. One factor that people argue about related to genetic engineering is who determines who has the right to select what is "favorable" and not. What do you think would be necessary to regulate the technology so that someone didn't, for example, genetically engineer an army of superhumans who could dominate a society?
2. Many people have previous ideas about genetic engineering from what they have heard on television or read in magazine articles. Think about the previous notions that you had about the issue and what you learned from these articles that you did not previously know. Did either of these articles change your position?

Is There Common Ground?

The future will ultimately tell us whether we will make a mistake either by allowing genetic engineering and tampering with the natural order of things or by dismissing it as science fiction and consequently watching many people die whose lives could have been saved.

It is reasonable to expect that genetic engineering will not be completely squashed as we progress in biomedical fields. Thus, we ought to change the discourse from "if" we will do so to "how" we can do so in a responsible manner.

Additional Resources

Nature Education. Human Genetic Engineering. Retrieved on May 21, 2013, from www.nature.com/scitable/topicpage/genetic-inequality-human geneticengineering-768.

Association for Reproductive Health Professionals. Human Cloning and Genetic Modification. Retrieved on May 21, 2013, from www.arhp.org/publications-and-resources/patient-resources/printed-materials/cloning.

Bright Hub. Pros and Cons of Genetic Engineering in Humans. Retrieved on May 21, 2013 from www.brighthub.com/science/genetics/articles/22210.aspx.

Internet References . . .

Genetic Engineering

https://www.britannica.com/science/genetic-engineering

What is Genetic Engineering?

http://www.yourgenome.org/facts/what-is-genetic-engineering

What is Genetic Engineering and How Does It Work?

http://agbiosafety.unl.edu/basic_genetics.shtml

Selected, Edited, and with Issue Framing Material by:
Kourtney T. Vaillancourt, *New Mexico State University*

ISSUE

Are Transracial Adoptions Problematic for Children?

YES: **Darron T. Smith**, from "Can Love Overcome Race in Transracial Adoption?" *Huffington Post* (2013)

NO: **Jessica Ravitz**, from "Transracial Adoptions: A 'Feel Good' Act, or No 'Big Deal'?" *CNN.com* (2010)

Learning Outcomes
After reading this issue, you will be able to:
• Describe some of the reasons that adoptions are necessary in America.
• Discuss the reasons that transracial adoptions might be preferable to institutional care.
• Discuss the arguments against transracial adoption, specifically what researchers argue the challenges might be.

ISSUE SUMMARY

YES: Darron T. Smith presents evidence from research that indicates that transracial adoption is not inherently problematic for children.

NO: Jessica Ravitz argues that transracial adoptions do not have to be problematic for children but does identify potential challenges that may be faced.

Our society has always preferred finding loving and caring adoptive parents for children rather than placing them in institutions. A family unit not only socializes a child but provides a child with nurturance, a sense of security, and unconditional love. Unfortunately, there are hundreds of thousands of children in America who, for various reasons, are not with their biological families. These children are mostly nonwhite, minority children. Although the research literature suggests that, regardless of the race of the parents or children, all children do better in adoptive families than in institutions, there still seems to be a "concern" about placing children transracially.

Transracial adoption typically refers to a family in which a minority child (e.g., Asian American, Native American, African American, or Latino) or a child with a mixed racial background is adopted by an Anglo-American couple. These adoptions account for about 15 percent of all adoptions in the United States annually. Due

to world events, transracial adoption became more commonplace in the United States in the late 1940s. Children with mixed backgrounds came from Europe and Asia after World War II. After the Korean War, Korean American children and refugee Chinese children were adopted by Anglo-American couples in the United States. Finding adoptive homes for Native American children followed. The movement to place African American children with Anglo-American families is the most recent evolution of transracial adoption.

The Multi-Ethnic Placement Act of 1994 and the 1996 amendments to that act forbade using race as a sole factor when determining if a family can adopt a child. The National Association of Black Social Workers strongly opposes transracial adoption because they believe the adopted child will have many problems dealing with his or her ethnic identity or ethnic community. Other organizations disagree and base their support of transracial adoptions on the principle of adoption being in the best interest of the child. The only time a transracial adoption process can be delayed because of race is if mental health professionals determine the prospective adoptee is a special case and an intraracial adoption is in that child's best interest. It should be noted that there is virtually no information related to the issue of minority families adopting white children. This has occurred, but only in rare instances over the generations. Although it is likely that the research literature would come to similar conclusions about the welfare of these adopted children, there is a need for research on this type of transracial adoption as well. At this time, it is not possible to say if society could embrace such adoptions without any "concern."

The following two sections describe the debate between restricting transracial adoptions and making transracial adoptions more commonplace via federal law. Despite the law, should race be a factor that is considered in adoption? Do you agree that attitudes and trends have changed and the controversy over transracial adoptions is no longer as large an issue as it was a decade or two ago?

YES ⤶

Darron T. Smith

Can Love Overcome Race in Transracial Adoption?

The recent explosion in transracial adoptions (white parents adopting black children) within United States, especially by high-profile celebrities such as Sandra Bullock, Madonna, and Angelina Jolie, sends an inaccurate message to ordinary Americans that race, racism, and the persistence of discrimination have all but faded from our national memory. And more so, that love alone is enough to raise a child of color. White parents that definitively espouse, "Love is enough" are doing a huge disservice to their black children. Research shows that black adoptees experience a high degree of uncertainty in deciphering the onslaught of race-based information (particularly with regard to self-image) they inevitably encounter in predominately white communities where they are raised; the adoptees often experience daily racial microaggressions that are typically "unseen" or misinterpreted by the white parent, thus leaving them exposed without developing effective coping strategies in a lifelong battle for their racial identity. The concern is not that these white parents are willing to love and raise a child of a different color, but that they are typically resistant to openly examining our nation's racial history and [identifying] their role as benefactors in a system of white privilege where white people receive a multitude of unearned, hassle-free benefits.

One of the limitations of white adopting parents raising black children is that the parents are viewing race through the lens of whiteness. In the history making of what it means to be white, this constructed lens is what white people use to view society and the world. This has been a privilege undeservingly bestowed upon whites in which they do not have to think about what it means to be a white person in society, but this poses a barrier to raising mentally and emotionally healthy children of color who will be confronted with their position in society on a daily basis. White privilege, which includes views on race through a white lens, stems from this nation's history of race and racism. Part of the challenge of being a white parent adopting children of color is comprehending the children's racial group history in relation to past and present. In order to understand racism today, one must examine its origins and evolution in history. To understand this is to gain some awareness of what a person of color experiences and the burden they carry for this country's past deeds. In that process, a white parent has to come to grips with racism and his/her place in a white racialized society. Only then can a parent begin to provide their child with the tools (tools that black parents tend to pass down as received wisdoms through mere experience) to have a strong racial identity and to contest the experiences and challenges they will surely encounter as a person of color in America.

. . .

The reelection of President Barrack Obama as the nation's first African American commander and chief emboldened the rhetoric among many white Americans that race no longer matters as a significant U.S. problem. The Obama presence in the White House only strengthens and reinforces in the minds of many that racism is nothing more than randomized situations where individual "acts of meanness" directed at one racial group by another play out. Through this mind-set, any one person can be racist, but most Americans see themselves as not racist. Unfortunately, these popular understandings of race are "normal" thinking that largely ignores our racial history of white-generated forms of oppression and violence directed at African Americans and other Americans of color, the aftermath of which can still be felt presently in our modern day society from school performance to the criminal justice system. Whether it's recoiling in the presence of a black man on an elevator, attending same-race church services or selecting a mate, race matters in virtually ever aspect of our lives.

Given that race remains is a salient factor in the lives of African Americans and other Americans of color, white Americans remain mystified when it is suggested that they are the recipients of unearned white-skin privilege that considerably shape the quality of their life experiences. The uncritical examination of race by white Americans and the perpetuation of the platitude of "color blindness" to succeeding young white compeers only forestalls any real efforts toward progressive change. As humans, we are generally not open to the idea of evaluating and correcting our personal shortcomings, particularly when it pertains to distasteful parts of our identity and self-image (or ego). Ask any African American or progressive white person and they will invariably tell you that white folks are not particularly receptive to robust discussions about the continuing problems of racial injustice especially if such discussions involve reparations or social justice as it pertains to black Americans. But fear of white offense and their subsequent silencing should not detour important moments of discussion with the goal of radically transforming our society toward a more democratic way, principally in the practice of transracial adoption where white adopting parents have an incentive and duty to rear physically, mentally, and emotionally healthy black children.

Black adoptees must be inoculated against white racial understandings, stereotypes and insults to black identity by well-intentioned and not so well-intentioned whites, and ignoring or de-emphasizing the needs of black children's racial identity development can have a profound effect on mental health. Black children need an outlet to discuss, process, and analyze race in ways that are both productive and protective for them. Because many white Americans hotly contest their own culpability in the maintenance of white racism, how is it then possible for white Americans, the most racially privilege group, to effectively teach black Americans, the least privilege group in our society, to cope with race-based mistreatment? In other words, how can whites' parents teach their black children how to handle being black in America?

In 1972, The National Association of Black Social Workers expressed strong reservations against the practice of transracial adoption for many of the reasons mentioned above. Although I strongly understand their viewpoint and agree wholeheartedly with their rationale, I also believe that white adopting parents have every good intention in raising their children with love. The reality is that the majority of black children in foster care will stay there until they age out on their eighteenth birthday, and I certainly cannot say that this is a better alternative to being reared in an all white context. However, I believe there is an additional alternative, and that is to encourage white parents to educate themselves and take ownership of their place in history and the unearned benefits they receive from a racist society. The recent death of Trayvon

Martin combined with the Tulsa killings should be a troubling wake-up call for those who thought racism was a thing of the past and particularly concerning for white adopting parents as foresight of what potential pitfalls their children may face by simply being black in America. By pretending that racism doesn't exist or suggesting it only exists in localized settings, parents are setting their children up for a lifetime of grief and self-doubt. Instead, parents must provide their children with cultural armor to protect them against the pervasiveness of daily racists' insults and practices. By giving your black children the understandings of our whitely framed world and the tools to handle this world, you are only preparing them with positive strategies to engage inevitable circumstances that they will encounter. There are ways in which white parents can gain understanding and skills that are useful for their black children. For example, read books by well-written, black authors on the subject of white privilege and white racism, move into more racially integrated communities, attend an African American church and other social functions, and finally, increase friendships with more African Americans of equal status.

I remain hopeful that white adopting parents have the desire, courage, and conviction to move beyond the racial frame that "race no longer matters in American society" and to recognize their own white privilege which represents a considerable stumbling block to improving the overall quality of experience of transracial adoption for adopting parents and children alike. However, if whites fail to take ownership of this problem in order to deflect any semblance of racism away from them, then we as a society further fail in our efforts to instill wholesale change.

Dr. Darron T. Smith is an adjunct professor at the University of Memphis, Department of Sociology. He is frequent political and cultural commentator and writer for *Huffington Post* on various issues of inequality in the form of racism, classism, and other systems of U.S.-based oppression. He has also contributed to various forums from Religion Dispatches and ESPN's Outside the Lines to *The New York Times* and Chicago Tribune op-ed sections. Dr. Smith's research spans a wide myriad of topics on including health-care disparities, Religious studies, Race & Sports, Transracial Adoption, and the Black Family. He is the coauthor of White Parents, Black Children: Experiencing Transracial Adoption as well as the co-editor of Black and Mormon His current book, When Race, Religion & Sports Collide: Blacks Athletes at BYU and Beyond, was recently released to critical praise in November 2016.

Jessica Ravitz

 **NO**

Transracial Adoptions: A "Feel Good" Act or No "Big Deal"?

"**W**hite people adopt black kids to make themselves feel good . . . A black child needs black parents to raise it." "Maybe she adopted one because the blacks in the community wouldn't step forward and adopt?" "What's the big deal? If no white person ever adopted a black child, they'd be saying why don't white people adopt black children." "Who cares what race they are? A woman got a child, a child got a mother . . . it's BEAUTIFUL!!! And yes I am black . . . if it matters."

These impassioned comments and thousands more poured in earlier this week when CNN published a story on the stirred-up debate surrounding Sandra Bullock's recent adoption. A People magazine cover photo of the actress beaming at her newly adopted black infant son, and the discussions that have followed, clearly hit a nerve.

So when it comes to transracial adoptions in this country, where are we?

Stacey Bush is the white child of a black mother whose adoption sparked controversy and whose attitude forces people to think about the issue differently.

Stacey wouldn't change a thing about her life, which is saying a lot for a young woman who spent her early childhood being neglected and bounced through the foster-care system. That was before a drawn-out legal case ended in 1998, allowing a single black woman, Regina Bush—the only mother Stacey had ever loved—to become her forever mom.

The Michigan lawsuit was filed when a county agency cited concerns about "cultural issues" in an attempt to keep the pair apart. Regina Bush's adoption of Stacey's biracial half sister had already been completed, without challenge, and Bush says she wanted to keep the girls together. (As a matter of full disclosure, this CNN writer's late father represented Regina Bush in the case.)

At 21, Stacey is thriving in college, well on her way to becoming an early-childhood educator and seamlessly moving between worlds. In one day, she might braid the hair of black friends, address faculty at Central Michigan University where she is on a partial multicultural scholarship, and then go salsa dancing with her Latina sorority sisters.

"People are sometimes startled. 'She's white, but she doesn't seem white,'" she says with a laugh. "I can relate to everyone. I like being exposed to everything. . . . Seeing me, hearing me—it doesn't matter what color you're raised just as long as someone loves you."

> It doesn't matter what color you're raised just as long as someone loves you.
>
> –Stacey Bush

Forty percent of children adopted domestically and internationally by Americans are a different race or culture from their adoptive parents, according to a 2007 National Survey of Adoptive Parents, the most recent study of its kind conducted by the U.S. Department of Health and Human Services. Legislation passed by Congress in 1994 and 1996 prohibits agencies getting federal help from discriminating against would-be parents based on race or national origin.

How adoptive parents have approached transracial adoptions has changed with time, says Chuck Johnson, acting chief executive of the National Council for Adoption.

"In the old days, meaning the '70s and '80s, there was this notion that these parents need to be color blind. This sounds wonderful, but by being color blind you're denying they're of a different race and culture," Johnson says. "Families that are successful are those that acknowledge race. . . . It's not a curse. It's not an impossible feat. They just need to work harder to give a child a sense of self-identity."

It may be ideal and less complicated to match children available for adoption with same-race, same culture families, says Johnson, who advocates that children be raised in their own countries whenever possible, too.

"But timeliness is of the utmost importance," he says. "It's better to find permanency and a loving home."

Ravitz, Jessica, "Transracial Adoptions: A 'Feel Good' Act or No 'Big Deal'?" CNN.com May 6, 2010. Reprinted courtesy CNN.

The latest figures show that there are 463,000 American kids in the foster-care system, of which 123,000 are available for adoption, Johnson says. Of those, he says, 30 percent are black, 39 percent are white, 21 percent are Hispanic, and the rest are of other origins.

Seventy-three percent of official adoptions—including those arranged through foster care, private domestic arrangements and internationally—are done by whites, according to the 2007 survey of adoptive parents. But that doesn't account for informal arrangements, when relatives take in other family members' children, which is much more common in the black community, says Toni Oliver, vice-president elect of the National Association of Black Social Workers. She says the black community takes in "more children than the whole foster care system does," although Johnson adds that often these arrangements don't have the safeguards and protections legal adoptions provide.

When handled well, transracial adoption is "a very positive thing," says Rita Simon, who has been studying these adoptions for 30 years and has written 65 books, including "Adoption, Race & Identity: From Infancy to Young Adulthood."

"But love is not enough," said Simon, a professor of justice and public policy at American University in Washington. "You really have to make some changes in your life if you adopt a child of another race."

In the case of a white parent adopting a black child, that might mean living in an integrated neighborhood, having pictures in the home of black heroes, seeking out other families in similar situations, attending a black church and finding role models or godparents who are black. The same need to integrate a child's culture applies across the board, whether parents are adopting from Asia, Central America, or elsewhere.

"It helps make our society more integrated," said Simon, who has five biracial grandchildren. "Race becomes less important and other kinds of identity issues become more important."

Bill Barry and his wife, Joan Jacobson, adopted two boys as newborns. Willie, 17, is biracial and Alex, 15, is black. Race never mattered to the white couple when they set out to adopt, after it became clear they wouldn't be able to bear children on their own.

"We simply wanted a healthy newborn," Barry says. "We didn't care about race, didn't care about sex, and we knew we wanted them locally."

Had the family uprooted to white suburbia, he suspects, the journey might have been more challenging. As it is, the kids go to public schools in Baltimore, Maryland, live in a multiracial and multicultural environment and grew up in a house where pictures of Paul Robeson and Rosa Parks hung on the walls. But Barry says he and his wife didn't "go way overboard." The white pair didn't, for example, suddenly start celebrating Kwanzaa.

"My wife is Jewish, though not so practicing, and we did Christmas and Hanukkah. Double the presents—they quickly celebrated that," he says. "Kids are always trying to figure out their identity and who they are, and race is just part of it."

That may be true, but the National Association of Black Social Workers has long argued for keeping black children in black homes. About 40 years ago, the association released a four-page position paper on transracial adoption in which it went so far as to call such adoptions "genocide"—and that word choice has dogged the organization ever since.

But Oliver, the vice-president-elect, says when that position was written decades ago, blacks were being discounted as adoptive parents, not being given the same resources to help keep families together and thereby prevent the need for child placements, and that agencies weren't recruiting families within the community. By speaking strongly, the organization helped jolt the system—although more still needs to be done, she says.

The idea that race doesn't matter is not true. We would like it to be true, but it's not.

The preference, Oliver says, remains that kids be placed in same-race households whenever possible. And if it isn't possible, or if a birth parent selects an adoptive family of a different race, then those adopting must be educated to understand "the impact of race and racism on the country, their family and the child in particular," she says.

"There is a negative impact that children and families are going to experience based on race," she says. "The idea that race doesn't matter is not true. We would like it to be true, but it's not." Regina and Stacey Bush have faced challenges along the way. They've received their share of stares and under-the-breath comments like, "What's this world coming to." When a young Stacey once started climbing into the van to join her family at an Arby's restaurant, patrons came running to grab her, yelling that she was going into the wrong car. The girl was given detention at school, accused of lying because she called a young black boy her little brother, which he was. At a movie theater one time, someone called the police because they feared Stacey had been abducted. Regina says she got attacks from both sides.

"White babies were a precious commodity. 'Blacks can't take care of white children,'" she remembers hearing. "And blacks were outraged" because there are so many black children in the system who need homes, and "they didn't understand why a black woman wouldn't adopt one of her own."

But she says she simply wanted to keep Stacey and her half-sister in the same home and give them a loving family, together.

Stacey says that upbringing taught her to embrace all people.

"It gave me so much opportunity to talk to so many different people. There were no limitations. I stood up for a lot of things, and it made me break peoples' mind-sets," she says. "We're accountable for each other as brothers and sisters. We need to look out for each other because at the end of the day we're all human beings."

JESSICA RAVITZ is a reporter and writer on the enterprise team at CNN Digital, where she focuses on longform storytelling and in-depth profiles, dabbles in first-person writing, and is often drawn to pieces related to health, women, faith, and quirk.

EXPLORING THE ISSUE

Are Transracial Adoptions Problematic for Children?

Critical Thinking and Reflection

1. Take a stance, pro, or con, regarding transracial adoption. Explain your position citing evidence from either the YES or NO selections to support your position.
2. What, in your opinion, are the two or three most important accommodations that adoptive parents ought to make in order to ensure that the adoption is a positive thing in the child's life?
3. What are "racial frames," and what role do they play in the issue of interracial adoption?

Is There Common Ground?

The Multiethnic Placement Act is intended to provide an effective support for transracial adoption. It seeks to eliminate the consideration of race in the placement of children except in exceptional cases. Legislation such as this is intended to protect the interests of adoptees and their prospective parents. However, do prospective parents usually prefer children of their own race? Or, are adopting parents pleased to have a child—of any race—to love and rear? Do you believe, as suggested in the NO selection, that as respect for all minority cultures and tolerance for diversity continue to pervade our society, the need for "best interest" legislation such as this act may become unnecessary? Will our society ever evolve to the degree that there would never be extenuating circumstances in which children placed for adoption need to be adopted by parents of the same race?

There are many children in need of adoption, and most are minority children. The goal of adoption is to get children out of institutions and orphanages and into loving and caring homes. The vast majority of the literature on transracial adoption finds little to suggest that it harms children when they are adopted by parents of a different race. The National Association of Black Social Workers seems to be the ones who are most vociferous in denouncing transracial adoption. Is this a form of discrimination, to prevent Anglo-Americans from adopting a minority child who is of a different race?

Although the efficacy of transracial adoption has been well established in the research literature, the controversy continues as to whether or not it should be widely practiced. Many feel that the issue should be laid to rest—once and for all—because children thrive more effectively in adoptive homes than in institutions. And, there are simply not enough same-race minority families to adopt children of the given race. Others suggest that although we as a society make overtures to being nondiscriminating, the practice still occurs in adoptions despite the law. Also, in some cases, people believe it is necessary to consider race in placing children. It seems clear that those on either side of the issue would agree, however, on two fundamental goals: (1) to decrease the amount of children in institutions and orphanages and (2) to place children in adoptive homes that will best meet their physical and emotional needs. The problem seems to be in the differing points of view as to how to best achieve these goals.

Additional Resources

Child Welfare Information Gateway. Transracial and Transcultural Adoptions. Retrieved on April 7, 2011, from www.childwelfare.gov/pubs/f_trans.cfm

This website defines and discusses reasons for transracial adoptions and expert opinions on their impact on children.

Issues in Transracial Adoption. Retrieved on April 7, 2011, from http://userpages.umbc.edu/~mmcman1/

This website discusses the various issues that must be taken into consideration when considering transracial adoptions.

Morrison, A. (2004) Transracial Adoption: The Pros and Cons and the Parents' Perspective. *Harvard BlackLetter Law Journal*, 20, pp. 163–202. Retrieved on April 7, 2011, from www.law.harvard.edu/students /orgs/blj/vol20/morrison.pdf

This is an article posted online that discusses some of the pros and cons of transracial adoptions, as well as the parents' perspectives on these types of adoptions.

Internet References . . .

10 Tips for a Successful Transracial Adoption

http://www.mashupamericans.com/family/10-tips-for-a-successful-transracial-adoption/

Transracial Adoption

https://www.pactadopt.org/resources/transracial-adoption-interracial-adoption.html

Transracial Adoption in America

https://www.americanadoptions.com/adopt/transracial_adoption

Selected, Edited, and with Issue Framing Material by:
Kourtney T. Vaillancourt, *New Mexico State University*

ISSUE

Is the Achievement Gap Increasing in America?

YES: Sabrina Tavernise, from "Education Gap Grows between Rich and Poor, Study Says," *New York Times* (2012)

NO: Rebecca Klein, from "Schools Are Finally Starting to Embrace This Method of Closing the Achievement Gap," *Huffington Post* (2016)

Learning Outcomes
After reading this issue, you will be able to:
• Describe what the achievement gap is, and what has contributed to its development.
• Discuss the connection between income inequality among parents and the social mobility of their children.
• Discuss how school integration is related to the achievement gap.

ISSUE SUMMARY

YES: Sabrina Tavernise reports on U.S. studies that show the education gap is growing between the rich and the poor.

NO: Rebecca Klein identifies a new method that schools are using in order to close the achievement gap.

The achievement gap in the United States is identified as the difference in standardized test scores, grade point averages, high school graduation, and college enrollment and completion, between children from different socioeconomic statuses and race or ethnicities. Research into the causes of the achievement gap has been conducted since at least 1966, when the Equality of Educational Opportunity "Coleman Report" was published. This report identified that home, community, and in-school factors are all contributors to the achievement gap. The findings of 1966 are of historical interest, and ideally, we would consider the achievement gap a thing of the past. After all, since we have known about the gap for over 50 years, one might assume that the situation for America's students has been drastically improved. That assumption, unfortunately, is inaccurate as we are still contending with an achievement gap and trying to identify strategies to successfully

close the gap once and for all. Until we are able to do so, children from differing socioeconomic statuses, races, and ethnicities are having very different educational experiences from one another.

For one example, according to Gandara (2008), Latinos are one ethnic group that is impacted tremendously by the current American education system. "Latinos are the largest and most rapidly growing ethnic minority in the country, but, academically, they are lagging dangerously far behind their non-Hispanic peers." The data show that 42 percent of Latino children who are entering kindergarten are found in the lowest quartile of performance on reading readiness, compared to just 18 percent of White children. These disparities do not improve as children progress in school. "By 4th grade, 16 percent of Latino students are proficient in reading according to the 2005 NAEP, compared to 41 percent of White students." And, the pattern continues to where in the 8th grade, only

15 percent of Latinos are proficient in reading compared to 39 percent of Whites. When we consider higher education, "only 11 percent of Latinos 25–29 years of age had a BA or higher compared to 34 percent of Whites." As if all of these numbers were not problematic enough, there is also the fact that "no progress has been made in the percentage of Latinos gaining college degrees over a 20-year period, while other groups have seen significant increases in degree completion." This one example highlights the gravity of the achievement gap problem.

Probably not surprisingly, the quality of schooling that children receive is not the only factor that contributes to the achievement gap. According to Berliner (2009), "extensive educational research in the United States has demonstrated that students' family and community characteristics powerfully influence their school performance." We know that when children have parents who read to them, who are in good health and therefore do not have excessive school absences, and who do not live their lives fearing for their safety or experiencing crime and violence, they have higher achievement. Likewise for children who "enjoy stable housing and continuous school attendance, whose parents' regular employment creates security, who are exposed to museums, libraries, music, and art lessons, who travel outside their immediate neighborhoods, and who are surrounded by adults who model high educational achievement and attainment will,

on average, achieve at higher levels than children without these educationally relevant advantages."

The existence of an achievement gap is not disputed, there is a substantial body of research to indicate that it is a real phenomenon. What is a point of contention, however, is whether or not initiatives such as No Child Left Behind are effectively closing the gap, or if the achievement gap is in fact getting worse.

In the following selections, the current state of the achievement gap is discussed. Sabrina Tavernese reports on studies that find that while the achievement gap may be closing between certain ethnic and racial groups, it is growing between families of different socioeconomic statuses. So, the achievement gap still exists but the parameters are changing. Rebecca Klein writes about a strategy that is currently being embraced because of its apparent ability to close the achievement gap, integration of different socioeconomic classes in schools. Both authors identify some positive areas where the achievement gap is closing, but also highlight that there is more work to be done. As you read through the articles, consider your own schooling. Where are the kids that you attended school with now, do you notice disparities in their achievement based on their socioeconomic status, race, ethnicity, etc.? If so, what strategies do you believe would have helped to minimize that gap in your own experience?

YES ↵

Sabrina Tavernise

Education Gap Grows between Rich and Poor, Studies Say

Washington—Education was historically considered a great equalizer in American society, capable of lifting less advantaged children and improving their chances for success as adults. But a body of recently published scholarship suggests that the achievement gap between rich and poor children is widening, a development that threatens to dilute education's leveling effects.

It is a well-known fact that children from affluent families tend to do better in school. Yet the income divide has received far less attention from policy makers and government officials than gaps in student accomplishment by race.

Now, in analyses of long-term data published in recent months, researchers are finding that while the achievement gap between White and Black students has narrowed significantly over the past few decades, the gap between rich and poor students has grown substantially during the same period.

"We have moved from a society in the 1950s and 1960s, in which race was more consequential than family income, to one today in which family income appears more determinative of educational success than race," said Sean F. Reardon, a Stanford University sociologist. Professor Reardon is the author of a study that found that the gap in standardized test scores between affluent and low-income students had grown by about 40 percent since the 1960s and is now double the testing gap between Blacks and Whites.

In another study, by researchers from the University of Michigan, the imbalance between rich and poor children in college completion—the single most important predictor of success in the work force—has grown by about 50 percent since the late 1980s.

The changes are tectonic, a result of social and economic processes unfolding over many decades. The data from most of these studies end in 2007 and 2008, before the recession's full impact was felt. Researchers said that

based on experiences during past recessions, the recent downturn was likely to have aggravated the trend.

"With income declines more severe in the lower brackets, there's a good chance the recession may have widened the gap," Professor Reardon said. In the study he led, researchers analyzed 12 sets of standardized test scores starting in 1960 and ending in 2007. He compared children from families in the 90th percentile of income—the equivalent of around $160,000 in 2008, when the study was conducted—and children from the 10th percentile, $17,500 in 2008. By the end of that period, the achievement gap by income had grown by 40 percent, he said, while the gap between White and Black students, regardless of income, had shrunk substantially.

Both studies were first published last fall in a book of research, "Whither Opportunity?" compiled by the Russell Sage Foundation, a research center for social sciences, and the Spencer Foundation, which focuses on education. Their conclusions, while familiar to a small core of social sciences scholars, are now catching the attention of a broader audience, in part because income inequality has been a central theme this election season.

The connection between income inequality among parents and the social mobility of their children has been a focus of President Obama as well as some of the Republican presidential candidates.

One reason for the growing gap in achievement, researchers say, could be that wealthy parents invest more time and money than ever before in their children (in weekend sports, ballet, music lessons, math tutors, and in overall involvement in their children's schools), while lower-income families, which are now more likely than ever to be headed by a single parent, are increasingly stretched for time and resources. This has been particularly true as more parents try to position their children for college, which has become ever more essential for success in today's economy.

A study by Sabino Kornrich, a researcher at the Center for Advanced Studies at the Juan March Institute in Madrid, and Frank F. Furstenberg, scheduled to appear in the journal Demography this year, found that in 1972, Americans at the upper end of the income spectrum were spending five times as much per child as low-income families. By 2007 that gap had grown to nine to one; spending by upper-income families more than doubled, while spending by low-income families grew by 20 percent.

"The pattern of privileged families today is intensive cultivation," said Dr. Furstenberg, a professor of sociology at the University of Pennsylvania.

The gap is also growing in college. The University of Michigan study, by Susan M. Dynarski and Martha J. Bailey, looked at two generations of students, those born from 1961 to 1964 and those born from 1979 to 1982. By 1989, about 1/3 of the high-income students in the first generation had finished college; by 2007, more than half of the second generation had done so. By contrast, only 9 percent of the low-income students in the second generation had completed college by 2007, up only slightly from a 5 percent college completion rate by the first generation in 1989.

James J. Heckman, an economist at the University of Chicago, argues that parenting matters as much as, if not more than, income in forming a child's cognitive ability and personality, particularly in the years before children start school.

"Early life conditions and how children are stimulated play a very important role," he said. "The danger is we will revert back to the mindset of the war on poverty, when poverty was just a matter of income, and giving families more would improve the prospects of their children. If people conclude that, it's a mistake."

Meredith Phillips, an associate professor of public policy and sociology at the University of California, Los Angeles, used survey data to show that affluent children spend 1,300 more hours than low-income children before age 6 in places other than their homes, their day care centers, or schools (anywhere from museums to shopping malls). By the time high-income children start school, they have spent about 400 hr more than poor children in literacy activities, she found.

Charles Murray, a scholar at the American Enterprise Institute whose book, "*Coming Apart: The State of White America, 1960–2010*," was published January 31, described income inequality as "more of a symptom than a cause."

The growing gap between the better educated and the less educated, he argued, has formed a kind of cultural divide that has its roots in natural social forces, like the tendency of educated people to marry other educated people, as well as in the social policies of the 1960s, like welfare and other government programs, which he contended provided incentives for staying single.

"When the economy recovers, you'll still see all these problems persisting for reasons that have nothing to do with money and everything to do with culture," he said.

There are no easy answers, in part because the problem is so complex, said Douglas J. Besharov, a fellow at the Atlantic Council. Blaming the problem on the richest of the rich ignores an equally important driver, he said: two-earner household wealth, which has lifted the upper middle class ever further from less educated Americans, who tend to be single parents.

The problem is a puzzle, he said. "No one has the slightest idea what will work. The cupboard is bare."

SABRINA TAVERNISE is an American journalist who writes for *The New York Times*. She previously reported for the Times from Iraq, Lebanon, and Russia.

Rebecca Klein

→ **NO**

Schools Are Finally Starting to Embrace This Method of Closing the Achievement Gap

It's about Time.

Socioeconomic school integration is on the rise, according to a new report from The Century Foundation.

Schools and states have poured millions of dollars into overhauling teacher evaluation systems, rotating staff members and collecting and analyzing data, all with the goal of helping to close the achievement gap between rich and poor students and lift the performance of struggling pupils.

But in doing so, many schools may have overlooked a proven educational innovation: school integration.

A new report from The Century Foundation, a progressive think tank shows an increase in the number of schools that have integrated socioeconomically and argues that more schools should be following suit. The report was accompanied by another study from the organization, which outlines the evidence for why racially integrated schools boost student achievement.

Schools have largely abandoned racial integration plans in the wake of restrictive Supreme Court decisions and public hostility toward the bussing programs that often accompany desegregation. But over the past several years, more and more schools have begun to integrate along socioeconomic lines, a method that often achieves the same goals of racial integration and is less constrained by Supreme Court decisions.

In 2007, The Century Foundation found that 40 school districts across the country took socioeconomic status into consideration when making school assignment decisions. Now, less than 10 years later, that number has more than doubled. Ninety-one districts in 32 different states now have socioeconomic integration policies.

Research shows that students—including disadvantaged ones—learn better in diverse classrooms. As the country becomes increasingly stratified by class, these programs can help boost the achievement of low-income students.

While 91 of the thousands of districts around the country might seem like a small ratio, "the fact that there are 91 [socioeconomically integrated] districts now is a massive change," said Kimberly Quick, an author of the study and a policy associate at The Century Foundation. "It shows really promising and encouraging momentum."

"At the same time, we know concentrated poverty has increased between schools and districts," she added. "In order to make the types of differences we really need, we'd like to see that number really expand."

Socioeconomic integration is less politically fraught than racial integration because it is often pursued voluntarily, says the report. In a number of socioeconomically integrated districts, parents can opt to send their children to intentionally integrated schools via school choice programs. Other districts have integrated by tweaking attendance zone boundaries.

"From individual conversations I had with either school board members or superintendents and deputy superintendents, they did not seem to experience the sort of intense pushback that happened when we tried to integrate schools racially," said Quick.

The idea of socioeconomic integration, Quick speculates, is more publicly palatable than racial integration, even as the two concepts remain linked.

"Unfortunately, as many wonderful images and stories as we have of racial integration, we're plagued by this negative imagery," said Quick. "What people can get behind is equity for all children. It's not as divisive as talking about race. Whether that's a good or bad thing, that's up for debate."

The federal government has taken notice of these attitude changes. President Barack Obama's proposed 2017 budget includes over $100 million to distribute to schools looking to integrate socioeconomically.

REBECCA KLEIN is the education reporter for *HuffPost*, focusing on K-12 issues.

EXPLORING THE ISSUE

Is the Achievement Gap Increasing in America?

Critical Thinking and Reflection

1. How would you describe the "achievement gap" to someone who was unfamiliar with the concept? What are some of the different variables that impact this gap?
2. What are some of the strategies that parents can engage in at home that can help to increase their child(ren)'s achievement in education?
3. If you were in charge of the Department of Education, what would you propose as a way of narrowing, or even eliminating, the achievement gap in America?

Is There Common Ground?

There is no disputing that the achievement gap is real, but there is some debate about whether it is increasing or decreasing, and what strategies would be most effective in finally closing the gap altogether. Tavernese's article reminds us that the problem is complicated and multifaceted. While we have seen improvements in some areas of achievement, other areas, such as the "rich versus poor" paradigm have grown. Because the nature of the gap seems to be shifting, there is a need to also shift the approach that we take.

Klein does not dispute that the achievement gap is real but reports on a strategy that appears to be effective in closing the gap, school integration. For some of you, integration may sound like an outdated term that was used during the racially complicated past in America, but there are still many schools and school districts in the country that do not draw from diverse populations (especially socioeconomic diversity) when making school assignments. This solution may not completely close the gap, but the research appears to support the notion that it would make tremendous strides in doing so.

Additional Resources

International tests show achievement gaps in all countries, with big gains for U.S. disadvantaged students http://www.epi.org/blog/international-tests-achievement-gaps-gains-american-students/

Poverty and Potential: Out-of-School Factors and School Success http://nepc.colorado.edu/files/PB-Berliner-NON-SCHOOL.pdf

Internet References . . .

Strategies for closing the achievement gap

http://www.nea.org/home/13550.htm

Racial and ethnic achievement gaps

http://cepa.stanford.edu/educational-opportunity-monitoring-project/achievement-gaps/race/

The Crisis in the Education of Latino Students

http://www.nea.org/home/17404.htm

Unit 2

Early Childhood

*T*he period of early childhood is sometimes referred to as the preschool years. It generally encompasses ages two or three through four or five.

This is a time when children become much more adept at taking part in physical activities, satisfying curiosities, and learning from experience. It is also a time when parents who think they have finally figured their children out realize that they have to adapt what they have been doing and learn new skills to deal with the new skills their children are acquiring.

Preschoolers play more frequently with other children, become increasingly skilled in daily tasks, and are much more responsive to people and things in their environment. Many children begin school during their preschool years, an experience that gives them their first extended contacts with a social institution other than the family. Changing attitudes about discipline, family size, divorce, and the mass media all have implications for a child's development. This section examines some of the choices families make in rearing their preschool children.

Selected, Edited, and with Issue Framing Material by:
Kourtney T. Vaillancourt, *New Mexico State University*

ISSUE

Is Spanking Detrimental to Children?

YES: **Rupert Shepherd**, from "Spanking Children Can Cause Mental Illness," *Medical News Today* (2012)

NO: **CTV.ca News Staff**, from "Contentious Study Says Spanking May Benefit Children," *CTV News* (2010)

Learning Outcomes
After reading this issue, you should be able to:
• List some of the arguments in favor of, and opposed to, spanking.   • Describe some of the negative effects that can come from spanking children.   • Identify the difference between mild spanking and physical abuse.

ISSUE SUMMARY

YES: Rupert Shepherd discusses findings from the American Academy of Pediatrics that state spanking can cause children to have an increased risk of mental problems as they age.

NO: CTV News Staff reports on a study that argues children who are spanked might grow up to be happier and more productive than children who are not spanked.

The topic of spanking, also known as corporal punishment, provokes highly emotional responses from family practitioners, parents, researchers, and children. There seems to be no one who is neutral about the subject, especially children. It would be interesting to ask children about their feeling toward spanking. Were you spanked as a child? What was used to spank you? Bare hand? Hairbrush? Ruler? Belt? The list could go on and on. Do you think the spankings negatively affected you, or did they teach you how to act appropriately? The following quotes are often used in relationship to spanking: "Spare the rod and spoil the child. I was spanked and I turned out OK. Kids need to be spanked to show them who's boss."

If you were not spanked, what was used to correct your misbehavior? Was the misbehavior explained? Was your correct behavior rewarded and your misbehavior punished? What about children who were not spanked or corrected in any way? Are they considered spoiled or out of control? Perhaps verbal abuse or a slap to the face was used to correct your behavior, or maybe you were ignored altogether. These techniques are considered similar to spanking in that they can become abusive or neglectful.

Ninety-four percent of American parents report spanking their children by the time their children are 3 years old. Although spanking is a popular form of discipline in the United States, several countries have outlawed spanking and the physical punishment of children: Austria, Croatia, Cyprus, Germany, Israel, Italy, Latvia, Norway, Denmark, Sweden, and Finland. Proponents of spanking point out that these countries' rates of child abuse have not declined as a result of banning spanking.

Corporal punishment is associated with family violence and child abuse. These are the stories often found in the media about parents injuring or even killing their children as a result of physical punishment. Although the media exploits these situations and makes the public feel outraged that children are treated this way, one must remember these are extreme cases. Most families feel they use spanking judiciously and do not consider it abusive.

Ultimately, spanking is used as a teaching tool and a way to solve problems. Parents see children misbehave, look for a way to gain the children's attention immediately, and spank them. Parents believe that by inflicting pain, they are changing children's behavior and solving the problem of misbehavior. Opponents of spanking ask the question of how children will change misbehavior if they are not taught what *to do* versus what *not to do*. In addition, the message is sent that I am bigger than you so I can solve this problem by hitting you.

In the YES selection, Rupert Shepherd reports that children who are spanked have been found to have increased risk for mental disorders when they grow older. He purports that between 2 and 7 percent of mental disorders were linked in some way to physical punishment. In the NO selection, CTV News Staff in Canada reports on a study that refutes the notion that spanking is detrimental. In this study, physical discipline was associated with increased school grades, optimism, and ambition.

YES ↵

Rupert Shepherd

Spanking Children Can Cause Mental Illness

American Academy of Pediatrics, which is already opposed to using physical punishments on children, has released a new study today, backing their stance and reinforcing the belief that spanking children belongs firmly in the past.

The study, named "Physical Punishment and Mental Disorders: Results from a Nationally Representative U.S. Sample," is released in the August edition of *Pediatrics*, which is online July 2nd.

It states clearly that **children who are spanked, hit or pushed have an increased risk of mental problems when they grow older.** The research seems to show that the effect can range from mood and anxiety disorders to drug and alcohol abuse.

Afifi, an assistant professor of epidemiology in the Department of Community Health Sciences at the University of Manitoba, Canada, clarified to *USA Today*:

> "There is a significant link between the two . . . Individuals who are physically punished have an increased likelihood of having mental health disorders. . . . [the studies findings confirm that] physical punishment should not be used on any child, at any age,"

She goes on to state that between 2% and 7% of mental disorders found in the study were linked to physical punishment.

The study involved a large number of subjects with data collected from some 35,000 non-institutionalized adults in the USA. Around 1,300 of the subjects confirmed that they had, at sometime, or regularly been *"pushed, grabbed, shoved, slapped or hit by your parents or any adult living in your house."*

The aim was not to look at more aggressive physical or sexual abuse, emotional abuse, neglect, but rather to identify the link between light deliberate punishment and Axis I and II mental disorders.

Axis I is defined as clinical disorders, including major mental disorders, learning disorders and substance use disorders, while Axis II relates to: personality disorders and intellectual disabilities (although developmental disorders, such as Autism, were coded on Axis II in the previous edition, these disorders are now included on Axis I).

The study has been criticized, however, with Robert Larzelere, of Oklahoma State University, Stillwater stating to *USA Today* that:

> "Certainly, overly severe physical punishment is going to have adverse effects on children . . . But for younger kids, if spanking is used in the most appropriate way and the child perceives it as being motivated by concern for their behavior and welfare, then I don't think it has a detrimental effect."

His own 2005 research showed that when light spanking is used appropriately, rather than wantonly and where it only serves to back up non-physical discipline, such as talking sternly to the child or enacting some kind of punishment or removal of privileges, it does, in fact, prove very effective at removing non-compliant behavior.

He goes on to state that the current study "does nothing to move beyond correlations to figure out what is actually causing the mental health problems. . . . The motivation that the child perceives and when and how and why the parent uses (spanking) makes a big difference. All of that is more important than whether it was used or not."

This would probably concur with the ideals of many mentally balanced and well educated parents, who would do anything to avoid having to get physical with their children, but ultimately, in the appropriate moment, with the correct words and mood, find that spanking can be useful and not cause long term detriment.

Afifi's report concludes that the findings inform the ongoing debate around the use of physical punishment and provide evidence that harsh physical punishment, independent of child maltreatment, is related to mental disorders.

RUPERT SHEPHERD writes articles for *Medical News Today*.

CTV.ca News Staff  **NO**

Contentious Study Says Spanking May Benefit Children

A new U.S. study that has drawn criticism from rights advocates says children who are spanked may grow up to be happier, more productive adults.

Researchers at Calvin College, a Christian school in Michigan, surveyed 2,600 people and included interviews with 179 teenagers. They concluded that children spanked by their parents may perform better at school and grow up to be happier than those who don't receive such punishment.

Teenagers who were spanked up to age six reported that they were more successful in school, more interested in attending university, more likely to work as volunteers and more positive about life, the researchers say.

Psychologist Marjorie Gunnoe, the study's lead researcher, interviewed people between ages 12 and 18. The study examined their responses on a questionnaire concerning how they were disciplined as children, and compared the responses to their conduct as teenagers.

The study, which hasn't been published yet, focused on a number of "good" and "bad" behaviours, such as optimism about the future and anti-social conduct. Teenagers who were spanked between two and six years of age performed slightly better on the positive behaviours—but no worse on the negative measures—than those who had never been spanked.

Another finding was that young people who were still being spanked when they were in their teens, displayed behavioural problems.

The study was not intended to encourage parents to strike their children, Gunnoe reportedly said, but to dissuade government from banning the practice.

However, Grant Wilson, president of the Canadian Children's Rights Council, criticised the study and said spanking should be banned.

"Canada is a country that should have eliminated this quite a while ago," he told CTV News Channel. "If you look at the polls, parents are generally speaking against hitting children for the purpose of disciplining them."

"It is contradictory to say to a child 'it's ok for a parent, a big person, to hit you and cause you physical pain,' and then 'you should go out and play with your friends and not hit them,'" he said.

However, Andrea Mrozek, with the Institute of Marriage and Family Canada, said spanking children can be positive if used "appropriately."

"There's a certain age range where it's appropriate and in fact may even be necessary to prevent greater harm to a child," Mrozek said.

"When you have legislature step in and tell parents how to be parents, I think it's extremely detrimental," she added.

Spanking is prohibited in many countries, particularly in Europe. It's legal in the U.S. and Canada, under certain circumstances.

CTV.CA NEWS STAFF is Canada's 24-hour all-news network.

EXPLORING THE ISSUE

Is Spanking Detrimental to Children?

Critical Thinking and Reflection

1. Explain the effects of corporal punishment on the parent–child relationship. List and explain one positive and one negative reaction to corporal punishment.
2. Explain the connection between mental health and corporal punishment, according to Shepherd.
3. Explain the reasons that CTV says spanking may actually be beneficial to children.

Is There Common Ground?

There is a real debate over what mild spanking is and how it fits into the overall parenting discipline technique. Child development experts agree that reasoning, talking, and listening to children teaches them how to distinguish right from wrong and preserves their positive self-image. They admit this approach takes more time and effort but that in the long run, it is more effective and leads children to a better adjusted adulthood. What might be some reasons that parents do not report using these techniques as frequently as spanking?

There are authorities in child development who believe spankings, when properly administered and within the context of a loving home, are effective in shaping children's behavior. Most agree to spank from about 2 years of age until puberty and to only use an open hand and never use objects to hit children. They urge parents to explain to their children why they are being spanked. Do you believe that this can make a difference in the outcomes of spanking on children? Why or why not?

Are spankings useful and justified, or is there a fine line between spanking and child abuse? Is it likely that parents who spank will cross that line to abuse in the heat of the moment? Is it really possible to spank with appropriate force and with logical thought? Can studies on the effects of spanking be designed to answer these questions? With all the studies already conducted, methodology and definitions are still being debated. It appears that there are many critical variables that need to be quantified before conducting research on the subject. In the meantime, parents are presented with the dilemma of how best to guide and discipline their children from childhood to becoming responsible adults. If you were advising a parent, what would you suggest?

Additional Resources

Henderson, T. (2010). Researcher Says a Little Spanking Is Good for Kids. Retrieved on April 7, 2011, from www.parentdish.com/2010/01/05/researcher-says-a-little-spanking-is-good-for-kids/

This article discusses some reasons why a little bit of spanking can be beneficial for children

Hunt, J. (1997). The Natural Child Project: Ten Reasons Not to Hit Your Kids. Retrieved on April 7, 2011, from www.naturalchild.org/jan_hunt/tenreasons.html

This website lists reasons that spanking should not be used on children.

Shute, N. (2008). A Good Parent's Dilemma: Is Spanking Bad? Retrieved on April 7, 2011, from http://health.usnews.com/health-news/family-health/articles/2008/06/12/a-good-parents-dilemma-is-spanking-bad

This article posted online discusses research about the effects of spanking on children.

Internet References . . .

Parents.com

www.parents.com/kids/discipline/spanking/

PsychCentral

http://psychcentral.com/blog/archives/2012/08/16
/why-shouldnt-you-spank-your-kids-heres-9-reasons/

Selected, Edited, and with Issue Framing Material by:
Kourtney T. Vaillancourt *New Mexico State University*

ISSUE

Are Fathers Really Necessary?

YES: Gail Gross, from "The Important Role of Dad," *Huffington Post* (2014)

NO: Mary Riddell, from "A Child Doesn't Need a Father to Be Happy," *The Guardian* (2007)

Learning Outcomes

After reading this issue, you will be able to:

- Identify the arguments posed in favor of an in opposition to the importance of a father's involvement in a child's life.
- List differences that can be found between homes where fathers are present versus those where they are not.
- List changes in family roles that have occurred over the past few decades.

ISSUE SUMMARY

YES: Gail Gross discusses the important functions that dads fulfill for their child(ren).

NO: Mary Riddell discusses that while fathers can be valuable, there are circumstances in which it is actually favorable for a child not to have a father in their life.

There has been a dramatic rise in single-parent homes in the United States in the past 20 years. A more dramatic increase is the number of children being raised by men. Since the 1990 census, households headed by single fathers have risen from 1.3 million homes in 1990 to over 2.5 million in 2006. Because of this increase, an issue that has confronted researchers revolves around the necessity of the heterosexual two-parent family. Specifically, are both mothers and fathers necessary to raise children effectively?

Children need nurturing, guidance, and economic security. Must they receive these things from both a father and a mother? Some scholars argue that children need active involved fathers throughout their childhood and adolescence. If this does not occur, children may be more prone to involvement in crime, premature sexual activity, out of wedlock childbirth, lower educational achievement, depression, substance abuse, and poverty.

Other scientists question whether the ability to meet children's needs is gender-specific. Although few would argue that it is more challenging to raise a child in a single-parent home, well-socialized and successful children have come from single-parent homes that are male as well as female headed. Females head the vast majority of single-parent homes. In fact, there are over 10.4 million single mothers raising children in the United States today.

Another consideration is the increase in adoption by gay and lesbian parents in two-parent homes. Although children face emotional challenges in dealing with the prejudice associated with being raised in these particular households, one might ask how this arrangement works. Is there evidence that children need both a male and a female parent? Many scientists argue that there is little, if any, scientific evidence that both a female and a male must raise children.

As you read the following selections, consider your family of orientation. Was your upbringing an optimal situation, in your definition of "optimal"? Did the role that your father played, or did not play, have a positive or negative effect on your life?

YES ⬅

Gail Gross

The Important Role of Dad

While almost any man can father a child, there is so much more to the important role of being dad in a child's life. Let's look at who father is, and why he is so important.

Fathers are central to the emotional well-being of their children; they are capable caretakers and disciplinarians.

Studies show that if your child's father is affectionate, supportive, and involved, he can contribute greatly to your child's cognitive, language, and social development, as well as academic achievement, a strong inner core resource, sense of well-being, good self-esteem, and authenticity.

How Fathers Influence Our Relationships

Your child's primary relationship with his/her father can affect all of your child's relationships from birth to death, including those with friends, lovers, and spouses. Those early patterns of interaction with father are the very patterns that will be projected forward into all relationships . . . forever more: not only your child's intrinsic idea of who he/she is as he/she relates to others, but also, the range of what your child considers acceptable and loving.

Girls will look for men who hold the patterns of good old dad, for after all, they know how "to do that." Therefore, if father was kind, loving, and gentle, they will reach for those characteristics in men. Girls will look for, in others, what they have experienced and become familiar with in childhood. Because they've gotten used to those familial and historic behavioral patterns, they think that they can handle them in relationships.

Boys on the other hand, will model themselves after their fathers. They will look for their father's approval in everything they do, and copy those behaviors that they recognize as both successful and familiar. Thus, if dad was abusive, controlling, and dominating, those will be the patterns that their sons will imitate and emulate. However, if father is loving, kind, supportive, and protective, boys will want to be that.

Human beings are social animals and we learn by modeling behavior. In fact, all primates learn how to survive and function successfully in the world through social imitation. Those early patterns of interaction are all children know, and it is those patterns that effect how they feel about themselves, and how they develop. Your child is vulnerable to those early patterns and incorporates those behavioral qualities in his/her repertoire of social exchange.

It is impossible to overestimate the importance of dad. For example, girls who have good relationships with their fathers tend to do better in math, and boys who have actively involved fathers tend to have better grades and perform better on achievement tests. And well-bonded boys develop securely with a stable and sustained sense of self. Who we are and who we are to be, we are becoming, and fathers are central to that outcome.

Changing Family Roles

Only 20 percent of American households consist of married couples with children. Filling the gap are family structures of all kinds, with dads stepping up to the plate and taking on a myriad of roles. When they are engaged, fathers can really make a difference. He may be classically married, single, divorced, widowed, gay, straight, adoptive, stepfather, a stay-at-home dad, or the primary family provider. What is important is that he is involved.

The emergence of women into the job market has forever changed how society views the traditional roles of fathers and mothers. Feminism and financial power has shifted classic parenting trends, and today approximately 60 percent of women work. Add to that, the shift in marriage, divorce, lowered birth rates, and family structures of all types, and you can see the emergence of a softening and changing of traditional parenting roles. This transition in economics, urbanization, and sexual roles has led to more opened, flexible, and undefined functions for fathers.

Gross, Gail, "The Important Role of Dad," *The Huffington Post*, August 12, 2014. Reprinted by permission of the author.

A recent study by the National Institute of Child Health and Human Development indicates that dads are more engaged in caretaking than ever before. The reasons for this are varied, but they include mothers working more hours and receiving higher salaries, fathers working less, more psychological consciousness, coping skills, mental illness intervention, self-worth issues, intimacy in marriage, social connection, and better role modeling for children.

Further, children who are well-bonded and loved by involved fathers tend to have less behavioral problems and are somewhat inoculated against alcohol and drug abuse. Yet when fathers are less engaged, children are more likely to drop out of school earlier, and to exhibit more problems in behavior and substance abuse. Research indicates that fathers are as important as mothers in their respective roles as caregivers, protectors, financial supporters, and most importantly, models for social and emotional behavior. In fact, a relatively new structure that has emerged in our culture is the stay-at-home dad. This prototype is growing daily, thanks in part to women's strong financial gain, the recent recession, increase in corporate lay-offs, and men's emerging strong sense of self.

Even when fathers are physically removed from their families, there are ways for them to nurture healthy relationships with their children. For instance, recognizing the important role fathers play in daughters' lives, Angela Patton started a program in which young girls went to visit their fathers in prison for a father–daughter dance. It was a successful program that has spread across the country and helped not only daughters find connection, love, and support from fathers but also for fathers to feel important in the lives of their daughters.

When fathers are separated from their children after a divorce, there are many ways they can remain bonded with their children. Though divorce is traumatizing to boys and girls alike, strong, consistent, and loving parenting from fathers can help make the transition successful.

Thanks, Dad.

Finally, on this Father's day, it is important to recognize and reward dads for being there, and actively teaching important life skills to children. It is important to their children, and meaningful to dads everywhere when you say "Thank you, job well done." This, after all, is what makes life worth living. This is your true legacy: ensuring the health and well-being of your children, that future generation to be.

DR. GAIL GROSS, PhD, EdD, MEd, an American Psychological Association member of Division 39, is a nationally recognized family, child development, and human behavior expert, author, and educator. Her positive and integrative approach to difficult issues helps families navigate today's complex problems. Dr. Gross is frequently called upon by national and regional media to offer her insight on topics involving family relationships, education, behavior, and development issues.

Mary Riddell   ➡ **NO**

A Child Doesn't Need a Father to Be Happy

To say the young have the right to a dad is to ignore the fact that many don't have that option, yet still cope with trying circumstances.

. . .

While no one denies that stable and loving relationships benefit children, the "traditional family" is an overrated institution. Far from being an automatic guarantor of harmony, it is sometimes the last sanctuary in which bullying, abuse, and violence can go on in privacy. Many brutal crimes are common in family life and some, such as incest, are specific to it.

Equally, good fathers are an unmitigated asset. Even medium ones, who spend too many hours at Citibank or the dog track are useful. Bad ones—the drunk and the vicious—may be worse than useless. Yet traditionalists make no distinctions. To them, married life is an oasis of fireside Scrabble games and homemade scones; a vision so irresistible that one wonders why Duncan Smith needs to waft a £20-a-week bung to entice people to enter, or stay in, this idyllic state.

In a speech to the Institute for Public Policy Research, Nick Clegg touched on why such nostalgia goes relatively unchallenged. As he says, the language of family has been captured by the right. In their latest crusade, against a few hundred lesbian couples quite able to bring up well-adjusted offspring, church, and political campaigners argue that children "need" a father and have the "right" to one.

Take need first. Fathers are not essential to rearing happy, successful children, and nor are mothers. The First World War, in which 500,000 children were orphaned, marked the biggest loss of fathers in modern history, far exceeding today's exodus of dads who flee or are excluded from their children's lives because a relationship has foundered or because they never wanted any involvement.

No one argued, as they do now, that crime and educational failure are pinned to the disappearance of male role models. This is not only a dispiriting message to Britain's 1.8 million lone parents, of whom nine in 10 are women.

It's wrong. Last year, Peggy Drexler, of Cornell University, wrote a book saying boys from fatherless homes can fare better than those raised in nuclear families. Her research showed that women could equip sons with a sense of morality and masculinity. For that, she was deluged with hate mail, denouncing her as "a fucking dunce" and a "femi-Nazi" who should move her "dyke ass to Europe."

Drexler is actually married with two children, as am I. She simply recognized that her kind of life was becoming rarer and wanted to explore new family models. Her research showed that fathers are not a necessity. But are they a "right"? In the normal run of things, Tory hardliners are as likely to advocate rights as to urge that Fortnum & Mason be converted to a drop-in center for asylum seekers. Those who think adult human rights belong in the straight bananadom of Europe consider children's rights to be as outlandish as the wish list the disaster-stricken Montserrat islanders once put to Clare Short: they'll be wanting golden elephants next.

The "right to a father" clamor coincided, by pure chance, with the 18th anniversary of the adoption of the UN Convention on the Rights of the Child. Next year, the United Kingdom will be examined on its compliance, or lack of it, with the convention. The last audit, in 2002, found us gravely wanting. As things stand, we shall get another pasting.

Last week the Children's Rights Alliance for England, which I chair, produced a worrying report. In the fourth richest country in the world, a third of children are still poor. We lock up 3,000 youngsters and treat them pretty horribly. In one jail, on five occasions children had to be brought round with oxygen after being physically restrained.

Smacking is still legal, which means children have fewer protections than adults. At 10, every English child is as criminally accountable as an adult. And yet, in the family courts, children get hardly any say. Many of those involved in last year's 132,562 divorces in England and Wales might opt to spend more time with a beloved father, but the law and the government aren't listening.

The convention, however, stipulates no "right" to a father, simply the right to know and be cared for by parents "as far as possible." When families split, children should have direct contact with both parents, assuming it is in their best interests. That seems to leave plenty of scope for lesbian couples as well as loving fathers and the vast horizontal families of stepparents and half-siblings that make many children more tolerant, independent, and resourceful than my generation ever were.

But fluid families also mean children need the basic rights they currently lack to equip them for complex lives and to protect them when things go wrong. That is the language of family that Gordon Brown should embrace.

Yes, marriage and enduring relationships are good. Yes, other models work, too. We all know that much. But with hardliners and the churches warming up for war, the government is going to need a better narrative to fit the jigsaw of 21st-century family life.

First, though, there's Christmas, surely a time for familistas to be broader-minded. A story featuring pregnancy outside marriage, a distant foster parent and a conception too outlandish for the IVF clinics of Harley Street does not suggest the traditional father is indispensable. As even the bishops might acknowledge, Jesus seemed to do all right without one.

MARY RIDDELL is a columnist for the observer. Her interests include constitutional reform, family policy, criminal justice, prison reform, and foreign policy.

EXPLORING THE ISSUE

Are Fathers Really Necessary?

Critical Thinking and Reflection

1. What do you think is the best way to encourage father involvement? Give three reasons for your answer.
2. Why would Riddell call the "traditional family" an overrated institution? Do you agree or disagree with this presumption?
3. What are some of the important functions that dads fulfill for their children? Do you believe these functions have become more or less important in the past few decades?

Is There Common Ground?

What role does the father play in the development of a child? Is it the role of dad and what society says he should be that becomes important to the child rather than how the father treats his child? Or, is it that important? If the former is true, then anyone, regardless of how he or she treats the child, will be important to the child. We often see evidence of this phenomenon in dealing with abused children. No matter what the abuse, most children in this situation want to stay at home with abusive fathers rather than be placed in foster care. When confronted with "telling on" their fathers, children will not say what abuse occurred for fear of losing their father's love and being separated from him.

If it is true that the role of dad and what society says he should be is what is important to the child, the quality of interaction and events that children share with their fathers becomes critical to their development. Then why could women not play that role? Women can interact with children in nearly all the same ways that men can. Women can just as easily accompany children to baseball games, act as the soccer coach, or attend the school play, as can men. Thus, the question might not be "Are fathers really necessary?" but "Are men really necessary for the positive development of children?" To many, this would not only mean an assault on the role of fatherhood but would also constitute an attack on men in general.

As with most issues, extremes on either side make less sense than the middle ground. Child development experts would probably agree that the more adults, both male and female, involved in a child's life, the better. Having a variety of people in one's life brings a variety of experiences and an extensive social network that can benefit children throughout their lives.

Currently, significant research on fathering is being conducted. Soon, scientists will be able to make more definitive statements about how mothers and fathers influence a child's life. Perhaps, one can conclude that as a society, we are all responsible for fathering and mothering. This is especially true for families that do not have the choice of raising children in a two-parent home due to divorce or the death of a spouse. We must continue to strive to find ways to support all families so that children will experience the optimal growth and development that they all deserve.

Additional Resources

National Organization of Single Mothers, Inc. Retrieved on April 8, 2011, from http://singlemothers.org/cms/index.php

The National Organization of Single Mothers, Inc., is an organization dedicated to "helping single moms by choice or chance face the daily challenges of life with wisdom, wit, dignity, confidence, and courage."

Parade. Obama's Father's Day Speech. Retrieved on April 8, 2011, from www.parade.com/news/2009/06/barack-obama-we-need-fathers-tostep-up.html

This website provides the full text of President Barack Obama's June 21, 2009, Father's Day speech.

The Family Economic Strategies. Retrieved on April 8, 2011, from www.sixstrategies.org/

The Family Economic Self-Sufficiency Project describes six strategies that families, especially women, can follow as they move from welfare to self-sufficiency. See the "Setting the Standard for American Working Families" report.

Work and Family: National Partnership for Women and Families. Retrieved on April 8, 2011, from www.nationalpartnership.org

This public education and advocacy site aims "to promote fairness in the workplace, quality health care, and policies that help women and men meet the dual demands of work and family." This site includes a wealth of information about relevant public policy issues, including the Family Medical Leave Act.

Internet References . . .

A Father's Initiative

http://www.washingtonpost.com/sf/national/2015/05/16/a-fathers-initiative/?utm_term=.0b70101cc185

National Center for Fathering

http://www.fathers.com/

State of the World's Fathers

https://sowf.men-care.org/

Selected, Edited, and with Issue Framing Material by:
Kourtney T. Vaillancourt, *New Mexico State University*

ISSUE

Does Divorce Create Long-term Negative Effects for Children?

YES: Brittany Wong, from "7 Ways Divorce Affects Kids, According to the Kids Themselves," *Huffington Post* (2014)

NO: Sylvia Smith, from "The Long-term Impact of Parental Divorce on Young Adult's Relationships," *Social Work Helper* (2016)

Learning Outcomes
After reading this issue, you will be able to:
• List and discuss some of the problems that children of divorce may face.
• Describe resiliency and the lessons that children learn from divorce.
• Understand some of the complicating factors that make it difficult to determine definitively how divorce affects children.

ISSUE SUMMARY

YES: Brittany Wong describes some of the negative impacts that divorce has on children, even into adulthood.

NO: Sylvia Smith describes the impact that gender has on the effect of parental divorce for children and protective factors that can minimize the potential for negative long-term effects.

How does divorce affect children? Do they perceive it as positive or negative? How would their lives differ if their parents had worked out their problems and stayed together, even if only for the sake of the children? How do children from divorced families differ from those in intact homes—happy or unhappy? Do both groups have similarities, or are they significantly different? These are questions researchers ask when they study the effects of divorce on children.

According to some studies, children from divorced homes are more likely to divorce themselves. Other studies indicate that the quality of the home postdivorce is more likely to affect children's development than the actual divorce event. Is society setting children up for subsequent failed marriages by condoning divorce? Or is divorce simply a solution to the problem of choosing the wrong partner, giving individuals a way of correcting that mistake? Does the divorce spell disaster for children as they grow into

adulthood, or are there other explanations for the problems, which children from divorced homes might exhibit?

As the divorce debate evolved from the 1960s to the 1980s, some professionals viewed divorce as an acceptable alternative to living in an unhappy home, while others saw divorce as having devastating effects on children and the family. In the 1990s, a movement to do away with no-fault divorce also spawned a renewed interest in the effects of divorce on children. Family scientists, therapists, and researchers questioned the belief that children eventually adjust to the effects of divorce and that it is better for children to live in a divorced home than in an unhappy, intact home. In the 2000s, longitudinal data on divorce's effects presented conflicting conclusions with more questions than answers to the issue.

There are numerous studies on effects of divorce on children. Some show that children benefit from divorce while others show it is the worst thing that ever happened. On the positive side, children from divorced homes reap benefits as a consequence of their divorce experience, particularly if parents model responsible coping skills. Some children do better in a home without the constant tension and fighting found in an unhappy intact home. These children appear more mature, more realistic about life, and more flexible.

Problems for children in divorced families are well documented. For these children, parents split physically and legally but not emotionally. These family members might ride an emotional roller coaster for years after the initial divorce decree. One parent pitted against the other with the child in the middle is all too common for divorced families. Family turmoil may result in children doing poorly in school, beginning to have sex at an early age, and displaying delinquent behavior. Children have no say in the divorce but must live with the instability and confusion that occurs after the breakup.

If parents decide to divorce, there are things they can do to keep the divorce more healthy, according to family life educators. They suggest not putting the other parent down in front of the children. This helps maintain some sense of stability and civility for the children. Seek outside help for the emotional turmoil associated with divorce, rather than using the children as a "sounding board." Make sure any heated discussions with the other parent are held in private where the children cannot hear. Also, try to accept the other parent's new mate so that children do not feel they are betraying the other parent when visiting the new family.

In the following selections, arguments are made about the long-term effects of divorce on children. As you read them, consider personal examples that you know of and see if you can apply the information in the readings to those examples. What fits with your experiences or examples that you have seen, and where do you think there may be exceptions or additional factors that should be considered?

YES
Brittany Wong

7 Ways Divorce Affects Kids, According to the Kids Themselves

If you're a parent considering divorce, fear of the unknown can drive you nuts. How will this affect the kids, you wonder. Will their grades slip? Will they hate me for putting them through this mess? Is this going to scare them off marriage and commitment for the rest of their lives?

That said, hearing how actual children of divorce fared may quiet some of your worries. We've gathered seven of the most interesting responses from a Reddit thread asking kids with divorced parents to share how the split affected them in the long run. See what they had to say below:

They Acted Out at School, But Took on More Responsibility at Home

One Redditor said he already had bullying tendencies growing up. Watching his parents' marriage fall apart only made things worse.

"My parents divorce increased [my bullying] tenfold," he wrote, "But after a couple weeks, I started feeling depressed and became really quiet and shy. It was tough being 10-years-old and not understanding why your dad has to leave and why your mother cries herself to sleep at night."

The one silver lining to the split? He stepped up his game as a big brother. "My younger sister was even more confused than me, so seeing her scared turned me into a super protective and loving big brother," he said.

They Felt a Sense of Relief

Some said they spent their teen years wishing their parents would divorce. "My parents never got divorced because they're Catholic," one Redditor wrote. "That said, once she finally did leave him, I was relieved. I can remember thinking when I was a teenager that I hated him and wished he would just disappear. It was just a shame I had to wait until my early 20s for it to happen."

They Felt the Financial Strain of Living in a Single-parent Household

Another Redditor said money struggles were a constant in her household. After the divorce, the Redditor, his mom and his sister moved into a one-bedroom apartment and his mom worked tirelessly to make ends meet. Two jobs was the norm, but sometimes she picked up a third.

"It was all in order to give us a good life, which she absolutely did," the Redditor wrote. "We may not have had the best clothes or everything we wanted, but she always tried to give us everything she could, and we never went hungry."

Watching his mom sacrifice for her kids made him respect her more than ever, he said. "At the end of the day, my mom is incredibly heroic for raising us on her own. I don't even care that I barely hear from my dad."

They Played the Blame Game

Life as you know it changes when your parents split up. It's only natural for a kid to rebel against the change in some way, as one Redditor admitted he did.

"I went off the rails," he wrote. "I refused to take responsibility for my own actions and blamed them for everything. I bought into the pity and coddling of those around me. Typical childish response, I know."

They Struggled with the Divorce, Even as Adults

Waiting to divorce until the kids are grown and out of school doesn't necessarily make it any easier, as one Redditor's experience suggests.

"I was 29 when my parents divorced, and I'd been living away from home for almost half that time . . . but it still hurt," she said. "Especially because my father is a jerk who waited until my youngest brother turned 18 to officially leave my mother."

They Didn't Take Kindly to One Parent Badmouthing the Other

A Redditor whose mom had primary custody after the divorce said weekends spent with her dad were something she came to dread. "The hardest part was listening to all the crap he said about my mom. He still does it to this day."

She added: "My dad always told me that I was manipulative and playing games with him. It took me more than 18 years to figure out I wasn't a manipulative, game-playing control freak. I was the *daughter* of one."

They Were Happy to See Their Parents Thrive after the Divorce

One Redditor said her parents' divorce was "distressing" at first, but seeing how happy they were living separate lives convinced her it was ultimately for the best.

"My dad especially seems to be excelling at life now," she said. "He is more outgoing and independent than I've ever seen him. Before, we never had anything to talk about but now he likes to tell me about all the new things he's doing and all the friends he's making. I now realize that this is the best thing they could have done for themselves."

BRITTANY WONG is relationships editor for *HuffPost.*

Sylvia Smith    **NO**

The Long-term Impact of Parental Divorce on Young Adult's Relationships

When parents divorce, many people wonder—what will happen to the children? From a psychological standpoint, it is very likely these children may start to question and worry. They may lose faith in their current relationships and family in general. In some ways, time seems to stop for these children as everything they thought they knew has suddenly changed.

Many children will think the divorce is somehow their fault, even if their parents tell them it isn't. Their whole world seems to crumble, and they have no control over what is happening. Which parent will they live with? Will they get to see the other parent? How will things work at holidays? Those are the short-term questions many children of divorce have in their heads.

What Divorce Does

Divorce causes families to change, finances to change, and children often will become depressed, anxious, or seek outlets for their frustration or mixed feelings. They become known as "the kid from the divorced family." It's not a fun title. All of this can contribute to a shaky foundation in their life. They can get on a path of negative thinking for themselves. If a child's parents can suddenly divorce, what else in life is going to crumble?

As if that isn't hard enough, another important thing to consider is the more long-term effect that divorce has on these children when they are eventually adults themselves. In fact, it has been the subject of various studies. Is a child with divorced parents more likely to have rocky relationships in the future?

What Research Reveals

Long-term impacts of parental divorce on intimate relationship was the subject of a study by the National Institute for Health and Welfare and the University of Helsinki in Finland. In the study, researchers gave questionnaires to 16-year-olds who had divorced parents, and then again when they were 32. It gave insight into their thoughts as teenagers and again as adults.

They did find that children with divorced parents were more likely to choose the same path in adulthood, or they chose to never marry. This may seem a logical outcome, as children tend to follow in the footsteps in their parents. But the interesting thing was that the study showed that to be true in the women—not the men.

The study found that of the Finnish children they surveyed, the women were the most affected in future relationships. The study stated that divorce was associated with poorer intimate relationship quality later in life among the women studied. No such associations were found among the men of the study group.

Why would that be? Was it because these daughters probably lived with their mothers, and then saw more how much their mothers suffered during and after the divorce? Or perhaps without a strong father figure always in the house, she didn't have a good model of how to relate to a man or even develop the faith that there was a good man out there for her. It definitely is worth exploring further.

However, there was another important aspect to the Finnish study which was a major factor in the quality of these women's adult relationships. According to the study, those with a good mother–daughter relationship caused those women to have more self-esteem and satisfaction in future intimate relationships.

What does this mean? Children learn from their parents. When divorce happens, they learn that this is a possible outcome, for good or bad. As adults perhaps it's in the back of their minds as a possible option when conflict arises. Also, they could be less trusting of others because they know that someone could leave them. Of course, everyone is different, and many children of divorce go on to have healthy relationships as adults.

What's important is this: when divorce happens to maintain and further develop those parent–child relationships. For each divorced parent, this means allowing those relationships with the other parent to develop. So be sure to allow proper time for them to happen and encourage them in that relationship.

As the study indicated, it's important to keep those relationships alive not just during childhood but well into adulthood. Children, even when they are in their 30s, need the support of their parents. They need someone who loves them who can offer a listening ear and also give advice when relationships come and go.

Divorce is a huge life change, at the time it happens and then for the rest of the lives for those involved. But, it is possible to move on and have healthy, positive relationships in the future. Parents should be good examples of what a health relationship can look like, so the child has the motivation and model to engage in healthy relationships as adults.

SYLVIA SMITH is a relationship expert with years of experience in training and helping couples. She has helped countless individuals and organizations around the world, offering effective and efficient solutions for healthy and successful relationships. Her mission is to provide inspiration, support, and empowerment to everyone on their journey to a great marriage. She is a featured writer for Marriage.com, a reliable resource to support healthy, happy marriages.

EXPLORING THE ISSUE

Does Divorce Create Long-term Negative Effects for Children?

Critical Thinking and Reflection

1. How do you think the media depicts divorce in the United States? Do you think it provides an accurate depiction, a harsher depiction, or a sugar-coated one?
2. Based on what you read in these articles, how accurate do you think the depictions are?
3. Provide examples of movies, television shows, books, and/or magazine articles in making your points.

Is There Common Ground?

When parents find that they are no longer happy in a marriage, which choice is better for their children? Should they stay together to maintain an intact home for their children even though there may be constant conflict? Or should they divorce, creating two households for their children, with the hope that they will find happiness either as a single person or remarried to someone new? How will a remarriage, in addition to a divorce, affect their children? Obviously, there are no easy answers to these questions as the opposing selections clearly indicate. One thing researchers know for sure is that no matter what traumatic event happens to children, whether it is a divorce, death of a parent, or natural disaster, the support and modeling of appropriate behavior by important adults in the child's life is critical. Children who have someone to talk to, who will listen to and guide the child, can make a significant difference in the way children adapt to negative life events.

Perhaps the answer is in making sure parents never have to face trying to end a marriage by divorce. Authors from each selection disagree on the long-term effects of divorce but would probably agree on society making more

of an effort to strengthen marriage to reduce the incidence of divorce. Strengthening marriage by providing marriage education for adolescents would help children learn how intact marriages work. Information on how to deal with current issues of balancing work and family as well as how to deal with conflict could be taught. This education could provide needed support to young adults as they choose marriage partners and help them develop healthy expectations of marriage.

Additional Resources

American Men's Studies Association. Retrieved on April 8, 2011, from http://mensstudies.org

The American Men's Studies Association is a not-for-profit professional organization of scholars, therapists, and others interested in the exploration of masculinity in modern society.

Eleoff, S. (2003). Divorce Effects on Children. Retrieved on April 7, 2011, from www.childadvoA cate.net/divorce_effects_on_children.htm

This is an article posted online that discusses some of the ramifications of divorce.

Internet References . . .

Age by Age Guide to What Children Understand About Divorce

http://www.parents.com/parenting/divorce/coping/
what-children-understand-about-divorce/

Divorce and Children

http://www.aacap.org/AACAP/Families_and_Youth/
Facts_for_Families/FFF-Guide/Children-and-
Divorce-001.aspx

Helping Your Child Through a Divorce

http://kidshealth.org/en/parents/help-child-
divorce.html

Selected, Edited, and with Issue Framing Material by:
Kourtney T. Vaillancourt, *New Mexico State University*

ISSUE

Is Television Viewing
Harmful for Children?

YES: **Jeff Jacoby**, from "Silence That Idiot Box!" *Boston Globe* (2009)

NO: **Austan Goolsbee**, from "The Benefits of Bozo," *Slate* (2006)

Learning Outcomes
After reading this issue, you will be able to:
• Identify some of the effects that television (TV) viewing is believed to have on children.
• Discuss the reasons why some researchers believe that violence on TV is causing an increase in aggressive behaviors in children.
• Discuss the reasons why some researchers believe that TV watching has not been studied in the correct way to support the negative effects that are reported.

ISSUE SUMMARY

YES: Jeff Jacoby identifies the harm that watching television can cause children.

NO: Austan Goolsbee discusses a recent study that provides evidence that television viewing may not be harmful to children.

The debate over television (TV) violence rages on. Ask any group of people you meet today about violence in contemporary society. The responses will be remarkably similar. "Violence is in epidemic proportions. There is a lot more violence out on the streets now than when I was a kid. It's just not safe to be out anymore. We live in such violent times." The anecdotes and nostalgia about more peaceful times seem to be endless. The unison in which society decries the rise in violence begins to disintegrate, however, when one attempts to discern causes for the increases in crimes like murder, rape, robbery, and assault.

One segment of society that is regularly targeted as a contributing cause to the rise in violence is the media, particularly TV programming. A common argument is that TV is much too violent, especially in children's programming. It has been suggested, for example, that a child will witness in excess of 100,000 acts of simulated violence depicted on TV before graduating from elementary school!

Lower socioeconomic status children may view even more hours of violent TV. Many researchers suggest that this TV violence is at least in part responsible for the climbing rates of violent crime, since children tend to imitate what they observe in life.

On the other side, critics argue that it is not what is on TV that bears responsibility for the surge in violence. Programming is merely reflective of the level of violence in contemporary society. The argument is that while TV watching may be associated with violence, it does not mean that it causes violence. As an example, the critics suggest that we have known for sometime that aggressive children tend to watch more aggressive TV programming. However, does the aggression predispose an interest in aggressive programming, or does the programming cause the aggression? This is a question that sparks hotly contested debates.

Those who believe TV viewing is at least partly responsible for aggressive behavior in children want the U.S. Congress to more closely regulate the ratings, viewing times, and amount of violence that can be shown on American TV. Those on the other side of the issue point to the infringement on First Amendment rights of freedom of expression if such intense regulation is imposed on the media.

Other factors that contribute to the issue of TV viewing and violence are the types of programs and commercials that children watch. School-aged children are the most targeted when it comes to advertising. There are more commercial breaks per hour for children's programming than for other types of programs. Additionally, with the widespread access to cable TV, children can watch violent adult programming, many times in unsupervised homes.

Several organizations have emerged to address the issue of TV violence and its effects on society. The Center for Media Literacy provides practical information to children and adults by translating media literacy research and theory into easy-to-read resources. They also provide training and educational tools for teachers, youth leaders, parents, and caregivers of children. The National Institute on Media and the Family sponsors "Media Wise," which educates and informs the public, as well as encourages practices and policies that promote positive change in the production and use of mass media. According to their mission statement, they do not advocate censorship of any kind. They are committed to partnering with parents and other caregivers, organizations, and corporations in using the power of the free market to create healthier media choices for families, so that there are healthier, less violent communities.

The two articles that follow are typical of the debate centered around violence and TV as it affects children. As you read them, consider your own experiences with TV viewing, and if you believe the articles accurately depict the issues. Also, apply your knowledge of research methodology to what is being said, to critically consider the merit of the research.

YES ⤶

Jeff Jacoby

Silence That Idiot Box!

YOU'RE A prudent parent, and you protect your children from behavior that is needlessly risky or harmful. You don't let them ride a bicycle without putting on a helmet. You wait with them for the school bus, or drive them to school yourself. You wouldn't dream of letting them drink alcohol, and if you caught them with cigarettes, you'd go through the roof.

So why do you let them watch so much TV?

For turning brains into mush, you can't do better than television (TV). The "vast wasteland" Newton Minow deplored in 1961 is infinitely vaster now—a largely unrelieved wilderness of mindless, stupefying entertainment, where dysfunction vies for predominance with vulgarity, and where the insatiable hunger for ratings eventually overpowers every consideration of taste, morality, and intellect.

TV isn't called the idiot box for nothing. Even at its best it replaces engaged and active thought with passive and sedentary spectating, while at its worst it destroys children's innocence, inuring them to violence, mockery, and crude sexualization. TV is by definition a visual medium; it appeals not to the brain but to the eye. You don't have to study hypnosis to understand how easily the eye can be exploited to undermine alertness, focus, and good judgment. Just look at the dazed and vacant expression on the face of a youngster watching TV. Most parents would be calling 911 if their child drank something that caused such a reaction. Why doesn't the zoned out oblivion induced by TV cause parents to panic? Is it because they're hooked on it too?

"Television Addiction Is No Mere Metaphor," reported Scientific American a few years back, and the identity of the world's foremost TV junkies is no mystery. It's us. According to the Organization for Economic Cooperation and Development, American households in 2007 watched an average of 8.2 hours of TV per day, nearly twice as much as anyone else. And we are awash in TV outside the home as well. In gyms, bars, and airport terminals, of course, but increasingly even in public elevators, taxicabs, and gas stations. Many airlines now provide live satellite TV on individual seatback TV screens.

It's bad enough that American adults watch so much TV. That so many kids wallow in it veers on child abuse. Some parents speak confidently of "educational" TV, an oxymoron on the order of "diet ice cream" and "congressional wisdom." Children don't become educated from watching TV, and the more TV they watch, the less educated they usually end up.

Countless studies have documented the inverse link between devotion to the boob tube and achievement in school. Researchers at Columbia's College of Physicians and Surgeons concluded in 2007, for example, that 14-year-olds who watched one or more hours of TV daily "were at elevated risk for poor homework completion, negative attitudes toward school, poor grades, and long-term academic failure." Those who watched three or more hours a day were at even greater risk for "subsequent attention and learning difficulties" and were the least likely to go to college.

In 2005, a study published in the American Archives of Pediatrics and Adolescent Medicine found that the harm caused by TV watching shows up even after correcting the data to account for students' intelligence, family conditions, and prior behavioral problems. The bottom line: "Increased time spent watching TV during childhood and adolescence was associated with a lower level of educational attainment by early adulthood."

The baleful effects of TV aren't limited to education. The University of Michigan Health System notes on its extensive website that kids who watch TV are more likely to smoke, to be overweight, to suffer from sleep difficulties, and to have high cholesterol. If TV came in a bottle, it would be illegal to sell it to children. Yet on any given day, 81 percent of 8- to 18-year-olds watch TV, and they watch it, on average, for more than three hours. Even the very youngest Americans are steeped in TV. According to their parents, 43 percent of children younger than two—babies and toddlers!—watch TV everyday. More than one in four have a TV set in their bedroom.

Tell the truth: Would more TV watching have made your life better? It won't improve your kids' lives either. Do them a favor. Turn the idiot box off.

JEFF JACOBY is a columnist for the Boston Globe.

Austan Goolsbee

 **NO**

The Benefits of Bozo

Proof that TV doesn't harm kids

According to most experts, television (TV) for kids is basically a no–no. The American Academy of Pediatrics recommends no TV at all for children under the age of two, and for older children, one to two hours a day of educational programming at most. Various studies have linked greater amounts of TV viewing to all sorts of problems, among them attention deficit disorder, violent behavior, obesity, and poor performance in school and on standardized tests. Given that kids watch an average of around four hours of TV a day, the risks would seem to be awfully high.

Most studies of the impact of TV, however, are seriously flawed. They compare kids who watch TV and kids who don't, when kids in those two groups live in very different environments. Kids who watch no TV, or only a small amount of educational programming, as a group are from much wealthier families than those who watch hours and hours. Because of their income advantage, the less-TV kids have all sorts of things going for them that have nothing to do with the impact of TV. The problem with comparing them to kids who watch a lot of TV is like the problem with a study that compared, say, kids who ride to school in a Mercedes with kids who ride the bus. The data would no doubt show that Mercedes kids are more likely to score high on their SATs, go to college, and go on to high-paying jobs. None of that has anything to do with the car, but the comparison would make it look as if it did.

The only way to really know the long-term effect of TV on kids would be to run an experiment over time. But no one is going to barrage kids with TV for five years and then see if their test scores go down (though I know plenty of kids who would volunteer).

In a recent study, two economists at the University of Chicago, Matthew Gentzkow and Jesse Shapiro, came up with a different way to test the long-run impact of TV on kids—by reaching back to the distant past of the information age. When Americans first started getting TV in the 1940s, the availability of the medium spread across the country unevenly. Some cities, like New York, had TV by 1940. Others, like Denver and Honolulu, didn't get their first broadcasts until the early 1950s. Whenever TV appeared, kids became immediate junkies: children in households with TVs watched their boob tubes for close to four hours a day by 1950. And these programs weren't educational—no *Sesame Street* or *Dora the Explorer*. Nor were there any real restrictions on commercials during kids' shows (those came in the 1960s and '70s). There wasn't the same level of violence on TV, but in terms of kids-oriented programming, *Howdy Doody* was about as good as it got.

The key point for Gentzkow and Shapiro's study is that depending on where you lived and when you were born, the total amount of TV you watched in your childhood could differ vastly. A kid born in 1947 who grew up in Denver, where the first TV station didn't get under way until 1952, would probably not have watched much TV at all until the age of five. But a kid born the same year in Seattle, where TV began broadcasting in 1948, could watch from the age of one. If TV-watching during the early years damages kids' brains, then the test scores of Denver high-school seniors in 1965 (the kids born in 1947) should be better than those of 1965 high-school seniors in Seattle.

What if you're concerned about differences between the populations of the two cities that could affect the results? Then you compare test scores within the same city for kids born at different times. Denver kids who were in sixth grade in 1965 would have spent their whole lives with TV; their 12th-grade counterparts wouldn't have. If TV matters, the test scores of these two groups should differ, too. Think analogously about lead poisoning. Lead has been scientifically proven to damage kids' brains. If, hypothetically, Seattle added lead to its water in 1948 and Denver did so in 1952, you would see a difference in the test-score data when the kids got to high school—the Seattle kids would score lower than the Denver kids, and the younger Denver kids would score lower than the older Denver ones, because they would have started ingesting lead at a younger age.

From the 1966 Coleman Report, the landmark study of educational opportunity commissioned by the Civil

Rights Act of 1964, Gentzkow and Shapiro got 1965 test-score data for almost 300,000 kids. They looked for evidence that greater exposure to TV lowered test scores. They found none. After controlling for socioeconomic status, there were no significant test-score differences between kids who lived in cities that got TV earlier as opposed to later, or between kids of pre- and post-TV-age cohorts. Nor did the kids differ significantly in the amount of homework they did, dropout rates, or the wages they eventually made. If anything, the data revealed a small positive uptick in test scores for kids who got to watch more TV when they were young. For kids living in households in which English was a second language, or with a mother who had less than a high-school education, the study found that TV had a more sizable positive impact on test scores in reading and general knowledge. Evidently, *Bozo the Clown* was better than we remember.

So, sure, you may cringe when your kid knows every word of the *Wiggles'* tune "Fruit Salad, Yummy Yummy!" That's understandable. Watching TV has taught them many horrible songs, and for that you will suffer. But maybe you don't need to feel too guilty about it.

AUSTAN GOOLSBEE is an economics professor at the University of Chicago Graduate School of Business and a senior research fellow at the American Bar Foundation.

EXPLORING THE ISSUE

Is Television Viewing Harmful for Children?

Critical Thinking and Reflection

1. Because television (TV) is in virtually every household in America, is it reasonable to think that TV programs could ever be regulated? Explain your answer.
2. It is reasonable to say that there are multiple alternative explanations for children's outcomes besides just TV viewing. Which of the alternatives do you think contributes the MOST to children's development and why?
3. Goolsbee discusses some of the barriers to obtaining quality and definitive research regarding TV's impact on children. Discuss one or two reasons that you believe are MOST difficult to overcome, and then one or two strategies that could be implemented in order to help improve the research methodologies.

Is There Common Ground?

There are numerous studies on children who watch violent television (TV) shows, as well as on the amount of TV children watch. Some research suggests that children who spend excessive amounts of time watching TV tend to do poorly in school. Other studies show that children who spend moderate amounts of time in front of the set perform better scholastically than those who watch no TV at all. Children are more likely to be overweight when they watch TV versus playing actively. If children are watching TV to excess, they are not communicating with adults in the family and are not learning family values. Logically, there must be middle-ground solutions to the issue of children, TV viewing, and violence.

Ideally, society could move past this dichotomy of thinking TV as simply good or bad. TV viewing could be thought of as an active endeavor rather than a passive one. Parents could become more involved with their children as they watch TV by controlling the amount and type of TV shows their children are watching. Through modeling, parents could teach children to be skeptical about TV advertisements, point out the differences between fantasy and reality, and argue that the moral values being portrayed on the tube are different from values that are important to the parents.

Additional Resources

American Academy of Pediatrics. Smart Guide to Kids Television. Retrieved on April 11, 2011, from www.

fcctf.org/pdf%20files/Parenting%20info%20pdfs/Smart%20Guide%20to%20Kids%20TV.pdf

> This website provides guidance for parents on how to handle their child(ren)'s television viewing.

KidsHealth. How TV Affects Your Child. Retrieved on April 11, 2011, from http://kidshealth.org/parent/positive/family/tv_affects_child.html

> This website discusses the impact that television viewing can have on children.

PBS Parents. Children and Media. Retrieved on April 11, 2011, from www.pbs.org/parents/childrenandmedia/article-faq.html

> This website addresses the most common questions that parents of children under three have about television viewing.

The University of Maine, Cooperative Extension Publications. Children, Television, and Screen Time. Retrieved on April 11, 2011, from http://umaine.edu/publications/4100e/

> This website discusses the impact that television viewing can have on children, in addition to suggestions for what parents can do and alternatives to television viewing.

Internet References . . .

Action for Healthy Kids

This is a nonprofit organization formed specifically to address the epidemic of overweight, undernourished, and sedentary youth by focusing on changes at school.

The organization's goal is to improve children's nutrition and increase physical activity, which will in turn improve their readiness to learn.

http://www.actionforhealthykids.org

Family: Single Parenting

This Single Parenting page of ParentsPage.com focuses on issues concerning single parents and their children.

www.ivillage.com/parenting/search? q=single+parenting

National Institute on Out-of-School Time

Directed by the Wellesley College Center for Research on Women, this National Institute on Out-of-School Time project aims to improve the quality and quantity of school-age child care nationally.

www.niost.org

Selected, Edited, and with Issue Framing Material by:
Kourtney T. Vaillancourt, *New Mexico State University*

ISSUE

Are Children Who Are Instructed with the Reggio Emilia Method Better Off?

YES: **Spielgaben**, from "How Will Montessori and Reggio Emilia Impact Your Child?" *Spielgaben* (2015)

NO: **Lella Gandini**, from "The Challenge of Assessment: Scaling-up the Reggio Emilia Approach in the USA?" *Early Childhood Magazine* (2011)

Learning Outcomes
After reading this issue, you will be able to: • Describe the basic tenets of the Reggio Emilia Method of education.   • Describe the reasons that a parent may choose to enroll their child in a school that uses the Reggio Emilia approach.   • Identify the strengths of this educational approach, along with the drawbacks.

ISSUE SUMMARY

YES: Spielgaben identifies the benefits that the Reggio Emilia Approach can afford to children.

NO: Lella Gandini discusses the challenges, such as minimal evidence of results, that the Reggio Emilia approach faces in the United States.

One issue that receives frequent attention is what method of educating children is the best, the most effective, or if there is one "ideal" approach that is best for the most children. Popular approaches involve education at public schools, private schools, and home schooling. More specifically, however, parents and educators debate the approach that is taken no matter what the school context may be. One approach that has gained greater interest in American in recent years is the Reggio Emilia Approach.

The Reggio Emilia Approach, named for the town from Italy in which it originated, is "a movement toward progressive and cooperative early childhood education." What is arguably the most surprising thing about the approach is that it is not considered a 'method.' According to An Everyday Story (2017), "there are no international training colleges to train to be a Reggio Emilia teacher. Outside of the town of Reggio Emilia, *all schools and preschools* (and home schools) are **Reggio-inspired**, using an adaptation of the approach specific to the needs of their community. This is important, as each student, teacher, parent, community, and town are different. No two Reggio-inspired communities should look the same, as the needs and interests of the children within each community will be different."

The fundamental principles of the Reggio Emilia approach are as follows: (1) Children are capable of constructing their own learning. (2) **Children form an understanding of themselves and their place in the world through their interactions with others. (3) Children are communicators. (4) The environment is the third teacher. (5) The adult is a mentor and guide. (6) There is an emphasis on documenting children's thoughts. (7) There are hundred of languages of children that they use to interact with the world.**

For those of you who are reading about this approach for the first time, it may sound quite strange, and very different from your own experiences in early childhood education. And, it may bring about a lot of questions such as: how can one teacher manage an entire classroom of children who are on their own individual path? What are the costs associated with such individualized educational opportunities? And, how do we even know if this type of thing is effective if each child is doing it differently?

Considered an "alternative" approach to early childhood education, the Reggio Emilia approach has not gained the popularity like, say, Montessori has (and even then, it is arguable if Montessori has truly gained widespread popularity). However, there are strong advocates for the approach who tout its benefits, and as such it appears that it is worth further exploration.

Our first article lists in detail some of the positive benefits that the Reggio Emilia Approach can afford children. In the second selection, Gandini identifies the difficulty in assessing Reggio Emilia schools, and how that challenge can cause there to be a lack of proof regarding the outcomes of such an approach.

YES

Spielgaben

How Will Montessori and Reggio Emilia Impact Your Child?

In this article, we take a look at how Montessori and Reggio Emilia schooling can impact your child and the many positive benefits that come with these forms of alternative schooling. Watch out for our next article on how Froebel and Steiner schools will impact your child, to give you a complete picture of all the alternative schooling types are so that you can make an informed decision when it comes to your child's education.

What Are the Benefits of Montessori for Your Child?

There have been many studies done on the benefits of the Montessori Method of teaching, and the results have proven to be outstanding.

Montessori is a way of teaching that focuses more on personal development as opposed to exams, and this approach produces more mature, creative, and socially proficient children, scientists found.

Psychologists in the United States found that across a varying range of abilities, children at Montessori schools out-performed those that were given a traditional education.

Five-year-old Montessori pupils were better prepared for reading and Maths, and 12-year-olds wrote "significantly more creative" essays using more sophisticated sentence structures.

Some of the biggest differences were seen in social skills and behavior.

Montessori children showed a greater sense of "justice and fairness," interacted in an "emotionally positive" way, and were less likely to engage in "rough play" during break times.

Montessori is against the more traditional competitive measurements of achievement, such as grades and tests, and rather focuses on the individual progress and development of each child.

Children of different ages share the same classes, and are encouraged to work together and help each other. Special educational materials are used to keep children interested, and there is an emphasis on "practical life skills."

Children were tested for mental performance, academic abilities, and social and behavioral skills.

Angeline Lillard, from the University of Virginia, who co-led the study, said, "We found significant advantages for the Montessori students in these tests for both age groups. Particularly, remarkable are the positive social effects of Montessori education."

Five-year-old primary school children had higher scores in tests of "executive function." This is described as the ability to adapt to changing and complicated problems, and this is seen as an indicator of future school and life success.

Even though Montessori children were not regularly tested or graded, they did just as well in spelling, punctuation and grammar exams as those given traditional lessons.

Older Montessori pupils were more likely to choose "positive assertive responses" when dealing with unpleasant social situations, said the researchers.

They also displayed a "greater sense of community" at school. The scientists concluded that, "Montessori education fosters social and academic skills that are equal or superior to those fostered by a pool of other types of schools."

There are a number of reasons for these positive outcomes from the research.

1. Montessori Focuses on Key Developmental Stages

A Montessori curriculum focuses on key developmental milestones in children between the ages of three and five-years-old. Younger children focus on gross motor and language skills. Four-year-olds work on fine motor skills and completing everyday activities, such as cooking and arts and crafts.

2. Encourages Cooperative Play

Because the teacher does not "run" the classroom, students guide the activities they do throughout the day. This encourages children to share and work cooperatively to explore the various stations in the Montessori classroom. Children in Montessori classrooms learn to respect one another and build a sense of community.

3. Learning Is Child-centered

Children are able to enjoy a classroom and curriculum designed around their specific needs and abilities which allows them to explore and learn at their own pace and on their own terms. In addition, older children in the class work with the younger ones, so mentoring comes as much from peers as it does from the teachers.

4. Children Naturally Learn Self-discipline

Even though this method allows children to choose their activities during a day, there are still rules for the classroom that are constantly reinforced. This naturally teaches them self-discipline, as well as developing important skills like concentration, self-control, and motivation.

5. The Classroom Teaches Order

All objects and activities have exact locations on the shelves in the classroom. When children are finished with an activity, they have to place those items in the same place they found them. It creates a sense of order, which has been proven that children thrive in this orderly way. When there is neatness and predictability, their creativity comes to the fore and they can focus on the process of learning.

6. Teachers Facilitate Learning

Teachers act more like "guides" who facilitate the learning experience. Teachers take the lead from the children in the classroom, while still ensuring that the rules are adhered to.

7. Creativity Is Inspired

As kids are able to choose their own activities and work with them on their own terms, creativity is encouraged. They focus more on the process as opposed to the result.

8. Highly Individualized Environment

Kids are allowed to explore what they enjoy at their own pace. This naturally encourages them to try more challenging tasks and this actually speeds up their learning process.

9. Hands-on Learning

Hands-on learning is a big focus in Montessori schools. It is based on concrete, rather than abstract concepts. All the activities they do teach language, math, culture, and practical life lessons. They are encouraged to focus on activities until they are mastered and they are taught not to interrupt each other.

Montessori is a great basis of early education, as well as an education method for older children. They are well prepared for life, whether they move to a more traditional school when they are older, or even if they stay in the Montessori environment.

What Are the Benefits of Reggio Emilia for Your Child?

When *Newsweek* magazine recognized Reggio Emilia in the early 1990s as one of the top approaches to preschool education in the world, the ground-breaking philosophy soon became more popular across the United States, including in a growing number of public schools. Now, it isn't just limited to the United States, Reggio Emilia is popular the world over.

"The Reggio Emilia approach is an example of how teachers can engage children in creative and meaningful learning activities," explains Shyrelle Eubanks, senior policy analyst at the National Education Association. "We would like to see more young children in schools have opportunities to learn using developmentally appropriate approaches like Reggio." Those are pretty powerful words!

Sometimes it's considered slightly out of the box and unstructured, but it works, and we'll show you why.

There are also many benefits to the Reggio Emilia method of teaching, which will impact your child in a positive way.

Where does Reggio Emilia come from? Basically, it is an educational philosophy started by the parents in Reggio Emilia, Italy after World War II. The parents believed that the destruction of war required a new, better approach to teaching their children. They believed that children form their individuality in the early years of development. The program they developed emphasized respect, responsibility, and community involvement. Children were allowed to explore and discover in a supportive and rich environment where the children's interests helped determine the curriculum.

One of the key principles of the Reggio approach is the fact that children have rights when it comes to their learning. The child is put at the center and is treated as a "knowledge bearer." By valuing children in this way, educators put more emphasis on really listening to the children. Educators are expected to listen and give ample time and space to children to express themselves.

Children in Reggio settings are active constructors of knowledge, and they are encouraged to be "researchers." Most of the educational experiences at Reggio take the form of projects, where children have opportunities to actively participate, explore, and question things. There is also a very strong emphasis on the social development of children as part of a community and their relationships to other children, their families and teachers.

So why does it work?

1. Expressive Arts Are Important

If you know anything about the Reggio Emilia approach, you will probably know that expressive arts are one of the most well-known aspects of this form of education. The idea is that children use different ways to express their understanding, thoughts, and creativity. This type of thinking has been endorsed by many artists including Henry Matisse, who wrote a series of essays, titled *Looking at Life with the Eyes of a Child*. They do this through drawing, sculpturing, music, dance, movement, painting, and drama as well as pretend play, which helps them to express themselves.

2. Long-term Projects

As we mentioned earlier, children are encouraged to be researchers, and this schooling approach gives them plenty of opportunities to do just that through long-term projects. They work through real-life problem-solving with their classmates, and this gives them opportunities to think creatively and explore. It is mostly led by the children with some input from the educators, and as they are given this freedom, these projects help them to think outside of the box and come up with creative approaches to problems.

3. Documentation

This is another key element in the Reggio approach. It is used as a tool for studying children's learning. This

documentation focuses on the experiences that children are involved in and the skills they're acquiring along their journey. These documents reflect the interactions between teachers and children, their peers as well as their environment. This helps teachers assess their learning and develop their curriculum from term to term. Children are allowed to ask their own questions and discuss problems, which can lead the way for their educational journey. It gives them a sense of ownership over their own learning experience.

4. Relationships

The Reggio approach is very focused on relationships between the children, parents, and the teachers for constant communication. *Children benefit in being equal partners with, parents and teachers in the learning process.* Everyone works together to form a spirit of cooperation and building the knowledge banks of the kids. Social collaboration is also important, so that children learn how to work in groups and be part of a team. Parents are actively involved in the child's learning.

5. The Third Teacher

The environment and learning spaces are the third teacher is the Reggio approach. Classrooms are generally filled with indoor plants and vines, lots of natural light, and each classroom opens onto an open-plan central space. Access to the surrounding community is made possible with wall-size windows and courtyards. Photos of children's activities, displays of their work, and even transcriptions of conversations are displayed around the classroom. Everything is displayed at eye level, so that the children can see their own work and that of others. The idea behind this is that the environment that they're in is part of the learning process and will change throughout the year.

The Reggio Emilio approach has substantial benefits for children as they lead their journey through their education and become confident and skilled individuals that can face the future brightly.

We hope this has helped you to understand these alternative types of schooling and how they can have a positive impact in your children's lives. Now read about how Froebel and Steiner can impact your child.

SPIELGABEN is a website that offers "hands-on educational tools for homeschoolers."

Lella Gandini  **NO**

The Challenge of Assessment: Scaling-up the Reggio Emilia Approach in the USA?

The distinctive approach to early childhood education that was developed in the Italian city of Reggio Emilia is known and admired by many educators around the world. Yet, given its renown, the number of schools practicing a Reggio-inspired approach is arguably smaller than some would expect. In this article, Lella Gandini examines the challenges faced in assessing the Reggio approach in the United States—notably the demands for measurable proof of results.

Over the past three decades, the early childhood educational experience of the Italian city of Reggio Emilia, population 170,000, has created a worldwide movement. It has inspired educators in a variety of cultural, political, and economic contexts, testifying to both the high quality and the adaptability of this approach. Since I published the first article about the Reggio Emilia approach in the United States in 1984, I have encountered many hundreds of teachers at presentations and conferences and visited many schools inspired by the principles of the Reggio philosophy and practice. Interest continues to increase.

Yet this story of success also presents a puzzle for some people: why, they ask, has the Reggio approach not spread even more widely among schools in the United States, given the high regard in which it is held? Three main factors can be identified. The first is that Reggio educators have purposely not set out to encourage their way of working to be copied. Unlike some other educational approaches, such as Montessori, there is no prescribed written definition of what constitutes a Reggio approach, and no way to be officially certified as a Reggio Emilia school. Integral to the Reggio philosophy is a deep respect for place, culture, and social diversity, such that the overall approach is not codified into a rigid orthodoxy or intended to be instituted and observed in precisely the same manner wherever it may be found.

On the contrary, the local topography, climate, ecology, and human history should be considered fundamental raw materials for children's exploration. Dictating how educators should organize a curriculum built around the local environment, or how children should follow a set sequence of developing one specific skill before moving on to the prescribed "next step," has no place in the Reggio approach. It is, rather, a philosophy to be adapted in a way that respects new cultural and social contexts. There are many ways to create a Reggio-inspired school without compromising fundamental principles of the approach.

A second factor has to do with the question of "cultural knots"—a term used by Ben Mardell in the book *Making Learning Visible*, published by Harvard's Project Zero and Reggio Children in 2001 (Giudici et al., 2001). Cultural knots are deep-rooted ways of thinking and doing that may be difficult to challenge and change. To take one example, in United States, culture time is often divided into strictly scheduled chunks, with educators thinking of their days as fragmented into blocks of 30 min. The Reggio approach, in contrast, offers a much more flexible attitude toward how the day develops, with learning experiences typically running over considerably longer time periods. Educators in other cultures may need to untie this and other "cultural knots" before they are able to apply the Reggio philosophy in their respective contexts.

Thirdly—and this is the main subject of this article—there is the question of measurement and assessment. While private providers in the preprimary sector have substantial flexibility to adopt the approaches they choose, educational providers in the United States who rely on public funding must demonstrably meet defined standards to maintain that funding. Assessments of these standards have a positive intent, namely, to ensure that children are learning. But they can also generate fear of trying anything new. Teachers may understandably focus on ensuring that children know what they need to pass tests, often to the detriment of other learning.

There is a widespread and mistaken view that the Reggio approach is incompatible with assessments of children's progress. As this article will show, numerous examples testify to the fact that Reggio-inspired schools can pass assessments required to maintain public funding. It will then also describe how researchers are working to develop

Gandini, Lella, "The Challenge of Assessment: Scaling-up the Reggio Emilia Approach in the USA?" *Early Childhood Matters*, November 2011. Used by permission of the Bernard van Leer Foundation.

new methods to assess children, with the potential to persuade more schools to adopt the Reggio approach.

> There is a widespread and mistaken view that the Reggio approach is incompatible with assessments of children's progress.

Reggio-inspired Schools and Assessment

How can the Reggio approach—featuring children's construction of learning through inquiry and expressive language—be combined with a curriculum that demands specific outcomes and assessments that require demonstrations that children are learning according to defined standards? Several schools and even school systems have found satisfactory answers.

Some of these answers build on a distinguishing feature of Reggio early education: documentation.

In-depth documentation reveals the learning paths that children take and the processes they use in their search for meaning. Documentation helps teachers and children reflect on prior experience; listen to each other's ideas, theories, insights, and understandings; and make decisions together about future learning paths. A commonly noted feature of children in Reggio schools is their meta-cognitive understanding of their own learning processes. Documentation does not mean measurement.

Documentation consists of "traces of learning," but no trace of learning is limited in its interpretation to a standardized unit of measurement. Nonetheless,

---

The Reggio Emilia Approach

The educational journey of Reggio Emilia started with the spontaneous initiative of parents in the countryside who, at the end of the Second World War, built a school from the ruins with the intention of constructing a better life for their children. At the same time, Italian intellectuals were arguing that schools could and should be an engine for social change. A young elementary-school teacher named Loris Malaguzzi biked into the countryside of Reggio Emilia to see for himself what those parents were up to. What he learned led him to emerge as the intellectual and organizational leader of the Reggio Emilia philosophy of education (Edwards et al., 1998).

In the early 1980s, Malaguzzi created an exhibit on what he and his colleagues were achieving in their city. Viewers flocked to the exhibit, and soon it was on display in Sweden and other European countries.

In 1987, a new and enlarged version, "The Hundred Languages of Children," began to tour the USA. This exhibit led to further versions—such as "The Wonder of Learning," currently in the USA and in Japan—that travel the world over. The publication in 1993 of a collection of essays on the Reggio approach, also titled The Hundred Languages of Children (Edwards et al., 1993), did much to stimulate further interest, as have professional societies such as the North American Reggio Emilia Alliance, and those in many other countries, including for example the Korean Association for the Reggio Emilia Approach and the Ontario Reggio Alliance.

Just before his death in 1994, Malaguzzi established Reggio Children, a non-profit organization. The Reggio Children website (http://zerosei.comune.re.it/inter/index.htm) offers this succinct statement of fundamentals:

> *The Reggio Emilia experience fosters children's intellectual development through a systematic focus on symbolic representation. Young children are encouraged to explore their environment and express themselves through multiple paths and all their 'languages', including the expressive, communicative, symbolic, cognitive, ethical, metaphorical, logical, imaginative, and relational.*

The Reggio approach respects every child's potential for developing competencies. Educators provide multiple choices for exploration, support a collaborative and inquiry-based approach to learning, and favor small-group work and project learning. Two co-teachers work with the same group for three years and the school operates on a community-based management method of governance. Education is seen as a communal activity – a sharing of culture through joint exploration by children and adults who construct learning experiences together.

documentation may be used as a basis to reveal a child's competences and learning (Fyfe, in press).

For example, Chicago Commons is a charitable organization that administers programs for government agencies such as Head Start. Each agency establishes its own standards, although some offer a choice of ways to assess progress. For the Department of Children and Youth Services of Chicago, Chicago Commons' preferred assessment instrument is the "Work-Sampling System" (WSS). The WSS asks for evidence, for example, that four-year- old children show eagerness and curiosity as learners; demonstrate self-confidence; use classroom materials carefully; interact easily with one or more other children; and so on. An assessment is based on regular documentation of children's work that is stored in the portfolios, binders, and journals of the Commons preschool classroom. All this is readily compatible with the Reggio practice of documentation (Scheinfeld et al., 2008).

The same system used for assessment in this disadvantaged environment in Chicago serves equally well in the Fort Hill Infant–Toddler Center and Preschool, a private entity operated by a liberal arts college in Northampton, MA, serving the children of college professors and others from the community (Lees, 2011).

Chicago Commons personnel treat the various external requirements as challenges; they brainstorm to find creative responses compatible with the main focus of their program.

Other examples of such responses, including one by a state government, illustrate this point. After the Reggio exhibit visited Columbus, OH, in 1993, the Office of Early Learning and School Readiness of the State of Ohio Department of Education undertook a statewide and multiyear project to organize groups of teachers to study the Reggio approach and to exchange ideas and experiences about implementing it. Together the 42 groups, made up of over 500 teachers, put together an exhibit that brought the fruits of their experience to their fellow teachers and the tax-paying public of the state. These included the attitude they favoured for confronting the issue of having to meet standards:

> As a community of learners we know that . . . if we embrace standards as guidelines for facilitating meaningful experiences . . . then it is possible for school to be a place where emergent curriculum and content standards can coexist and children's research can come alive.
>
> (Shoptaugh et al., 2006)

At the Opal School in Portland, OR, a public charter elementary school that includes a preschool, staff members consider standards as resources rather than obstacles. They address the Oregon Academic Content Standards by "chewing on the big ideas found in the Common Goals, rather than on the bite-sized pieces assigned to each grade level." Children at this school score well on the required tests (Graves and MacKay, 2009).

Our final example is the Ochoa Elementary School in Tucson, AZ, just 65 miles from the Mexican border. Children are predominantly from low-income, Spanish-speaking families. Over three harrowing years, the school was brought back from the brink of closure for failing to meet performance targets under the No Child Left Behind Act. Instead of being left behind, Ochoa, by embracing the Reggio approach, became a model for others to follow. The school recently received a grant to become a Reggio-inspired Community Magnet school. Ochoa intends to follow the examples of and collaborate with the Opal School and Chicago Commons with regard to assessment (Krechevsky et al., 2011).

New Directions in Assessment

In parallel to these efforts of Reggio-inspired schools to address current assessment requirements, another approach is to find new ways to assess schools and children's learning that are also in keeping with the Reggio approach.

The effort to devise new assessment measures is being led by Making Learning Visible researchers Mara Krechevsky and Ben Mardell at the Harvard Graduate School of Education's Project Zero, and Karen Haigh from Columbia College, Chicago. For over a decade, these individuals have worked with educators in public schools to adopt Reggio-inspired ideas and to help children master basic literacy and numeracy skills. Nonetheless, the lack of child outcome data hinders expanding this work to other public settings that serve children from disadvantaged backgrounds (Baker et al., 2010).

The Project Zero researchers therefore plan to create authentic measures of critical thinking, communication, collaboration, and creativity in order to assess the impact of Reggio-inspired teaching on children's learning. The assessments will target three primary contexts: teacher-led conversations, child-directed activities, and structured small-group tasks. For example, the assessment of teacher-led conversations with children (whole or small group) will consider such questions as:

- How do teachers facilitate the conversation? Do they refer children to other children?
- Are new statements linked to previous ones and do ideas build on one another? Do children and adults listen to each other?
- What is the purpose of the conversation? Is it to share what children already know or build new knowledge? How do children structure their sentences?
- Do children help each other by providing critiques or explaining ideas to each other? How do they handle conflict? Do they use a language of thinking and emotion?
- Is there laughter and are there expressions of excitement and joy?
- The assessment of child-directed exploration in groups will focus on:
- What is the quality of the exploration? Given the children's ages and experiences, is the play scenario sophisticated and complex or more limited? Are the children open to multiple solutions?
- What is the quality of the children's interactions? Do they share ideas with one another? How do they solve problems and deal with conflict?
- What is the role of the teacher? How does the teacher respond to children's ideas and questions? How does he or she deal with conflict and issues of sharing and equity?

The structured, small-group task will involve a standardized activity where children will be asked to solve a problem (such as communicating to a new classmate the rules of the school) or use materials to create a product (for example, fashioning a present for the teacher). The group process will be video recorded and analyzed for the degree of collaboration and creativity. How the group communicates its ideas (for example, whether it uses some form of written notation) will also be assessed.

The quest for a new method of assessment, conducted thoughtfully, is undeniably worthwhile. The resulting data could provide the evidence needed to persuade administrators that Reggio-inspired schools are superior both in quality and support of children's learning. Whether this would lead to scaling without sacrificing that quality remains to be seen.

References

Baker, P., Aranda, H. and McPheeters, P. (2010). Becoming a Reggio-inspired public school: The Ochoa story. *Innovations in Early Childhood Education* 17(4): 6–19.

Edwards, C.P., Gandini, L. and Forman, G. (eds.) (1993). *The Hundred Languages of Children: The Reggio Emilia approach to early childhood education.* Westport, CT: Ablex/Greenwood.

Edwards, C.P., Gandini, L. and Forman, G. (eds.) (1998). *The Hundred Languages of Children: Advanced reflections,* 2nd edn. Westport, CT: Ablex/Greenwood.

Fyfe, B. (in press). The relationship between documentation and assessment. In: Edwards, C.P., Gandini, L. and Forman, G. (eds) *The Hundred Languages Of Children: The Reggio experience in transformation,* 3rd edn. Westport, CT: Praeger.

Giudici, C., Rinaldi, C. and Krechevsky, M. (eds). (2001). *Making Learning Visible: Children as individual and group learners.* Reggio Emilia: Reggio Children and Harvard College.

Graves, J. and MacKay, S. (2009). One school's response to state standards. *Innovations in Early Childhood Education* 16(1): 10–17.

Krechevsky, M., Mardell, B., Rivard, M. and Haigh, K. (2011). *Promoting 21st-century Learners, Right from the Start.* Unpublished manuscript.

Lees, M. (2011). Personal communication, 19 August. Northampton, MA: Smith College Center for Early Childhood.

Scheinfeld, D., Haigh, K. and Scheinfeld, S. (2008). *We Are All Explorers: Learning and teaching with Reggio principles in urban settings.* New York, NY: Teachers College Press.

Shoptaugh, S., Frasier, B., Miller, S., Bardwell, A. and Bersani, C. (2006). The importance of educational exchange: A state-wide initiative. *Innovations in Early Childhood Education* 13(3): 12–21.

LELLA GANDINI is a United States Liaison for the Reggio Emilia Program in the United States and an adjunct professor at the University of Massachusetts, Amherst.

EXPLORING THE ISSUE

Are Children Who Are Instructed with the Reggio Emilia Method Better Off?

Critical Thinking and Reflection

1. Describe the basic principles of the Reggio Emilia approach, and how are they similar, and different, than more traditional educational approaches?
2. When considering what type of school that a child should attend, what are important factors for parents to consider?
3. What do you believe are some of the barriers that are in place that have kept the Reggio Emilia Approach from growing in popularity in America when compared to other educational approaches?

Is There Common Ground?

The goal of early childhood education is to provide children with a solid foundation upon which to build academic and social skills. There is no one way that fits for every child, and certainly, no one way that everyone agrees is the "best" approach to take. Not only do parents have to consider what they believe to be the best approach for their child(ren), they also have to contend with constraints, such as financial limitations or lack of access, that can prohibit them from enrolling their children in the program that they would prefer.

For some children, the Reggio Emilia approach appears to be a great fit, providing for their needs and helping them to grow and learn in the best possible way. Currently in America, however, the majority of early childhood education is provided through public schooling that engages in a more "traditional" method of instruction. Would it be possible, or appropriate, for public schools to embrace some of the principles of the Reggio Emilia approach? Or, would that require too many resources to

be successful? Only time will tell, of course, but as research continues to be conducted and the efficacy of "alternative" approaches are assessed, perhaps there is room in the dialogue for greater consideration to expand our current repertoire.

Additional Resources

Hewitt, Valarie (2001). "Examining the Reggio Emilia Approach to Early Childhood Education." *Early Childhood Education Journal*. **29** (2): 95–10.

Katz, Lilian (1993). Edwards, C.; Gandini, L.; Forman, G., eds. *The Hundred Languages of Children: The Reggio Emilia Approach to Early Childhood Education*. Norwood, NJ: Ablex Publishing Corporation. pp. 19–37.

Baldini, Belpoliti, Bonilauri, Bruner, Cavazzoni, T. Filippini, Rinaldi, Vecchi, Zini, Davoli, Ferri. *Reggio Tutta, a guide to the city by the children*. Reggio Children 2000

Internet References . . .

Be Reggio Inspired

http://www.letthechildrenplay.net/2013/03/be-reggio-
inspired-indoor-learning.html

What Is the Reggio Emilia Approach?

http://www.aneverydaystory.com/beginners-guide-to-
reggio-emilia/main-principles/

What Is the Reggio Emilia Approach?

https://childdiscoverycenter.org/non-traditional-
classroom/what-is-the-reggio-emilia-approach/

Unit 3

UNIT

Middle Childhood

*M*iddle childhood, or school age, is the period from ages five through twelve. The rate of a child's growth that has been relatively steady prior to this point generally declines until the later part of this stage of development. Perhaps the most important experience during middle childhood is schooling.

As a child progresses through this stage, new significant others outside the family emerge in the child's life. Children gain a broader understanding of the similarities and differences among them. The peer group (especially same-sex peers), teachers, and media personalities take on increased importance for the child. This section examines issues related to schooling, language development, and self-care.

Selected, Edited, and with Issue Framing Material by:
Kourtney T. Vaillancourt, *New Mexico State University*

ISSUE

Does Marriage Impact the Well-being of Children?

YES: W. Bradford Wilcox, from "Marriage Makes Our Children Richer—Here's Why," *The Atlantic* (2013)

NO: Nancy Pina, from "3 Ways Your Unhappy Marriage May Be Hurting Your Kids," *Huffington Post* (2014)

Learning Outcomes
After reading this issue, you will be able to:
• List and discuss the benefits of marriage that researchers have identified.
• List some of the ways that the well-being of children can be improved.
• Discuss some of the reasons that marriage is considered to not be beneficial to the well-being of children.

ISSUE SUMMARY

YES: W. Bradford Wilcox describes how healthy and happy marriages impact the well-being of children.

NO: Nancy Pina discusses how marriage alone is not a protective factor for children, if there is unhappiness between spouses.

There is no doubt that living with two parents who are married and who want to be together is good for children, psychologically and economically. Having two married parents means that there is a possibility for two incomes, which would provide a higher standard of living for children and would make it more likely that the children will not grow up in poverty. Presently, the majority of children living in poverty live with a single parent, usually their mom.

And yet, is the issue that simple? Should we merely request or require that parents marry? Will that make everything all right? Will children's well-being improve if their parents get married? One-third of poor children live within a two-parent family. If the premise that marriage improves well-being for children is true, what happened to these families?

The complicated issue involving the living standards of children and marriage promotion has become intertwined with the issues of welfare reform. As welfare reform has evolved, funding for Temporary Assistance for Needy Families has also changed. While improving living standards for children has always been states' prominent goal, by moving families from welfare to work, states have been allowed to choose their own method of using federal dollars to accomplish this goal. The individuation of states has complicated this issue. Some states choose to provide affordable childcare, education, and job training as a way to move families from welfare to work, and in so doing, they have managed to improve living standards for children. With the marriage promotion initiative, states that show higher levels of marriage rates receive more federal dollars for the welfare reform initiative. Although there is no empirical evidence that this type of programming works, states are likely to adopt programs that promote marriage, regardless of whether or not these programs are effective in improving living standards and well-being for children. Some states do this merely to increase funding levels.

YES ↵

W. Bradford Wilcox

Marriage Makes Our Children Richer—Here's Why

Young people from less-privileged homes are more likely to graduate from college and earn more if raised by two married parents.

The United States' reputation as "the land of opportunity" is a cruel bit of false advertising.

Americans are less likely to experience relative economic mobility than our peers in countries like Canada, Denmark, and Sweden. Children born to poor and working-class parents are considerably less likely to reach the highest rungs of the economic ladder than their richer classmates.

But why? One of the most promising new groups working to answer this question is Opportunity Nation, a group committed to working across partisan and ideological lines "to expand economic opportunity and close the opportunity gap in America." Their newly released Opportunity Index includes 16 indicators, from high-school graduation to income inequality. But not one indicator relates to the family.

Young adults are 44 percent more likely to have graduated from college if they were raised by their married parents.

In fact, the opportunity story begins with our families—in particular, with our parents. As the Nobel-prize-winning economist James Heckman recently noted, "the family into which a child is born plays a powerful role in determining lifetime opportunities." My own research using individual-level data from the Add Health data set for the Home Economics Project, a new joint initiative between the American Enterprise Institute and the Institute for Family Studies, indicates that adolescents raised in intact, married homes are significantly more likely to succeed educationally and financially. The benefits are greatest for less privileged homes—that is, where their mother did not have a college degree.

As the next graph indicates, young men and women who hail from intact, married homes are much more likely to graduate from college. More precisely, young adults are at least 44 percent more likely to have graduated from college if they were raised by their married parents. This is important because a college degree is associated with better work opportunities, lower odds of unemployment, and a substantial wage premium.

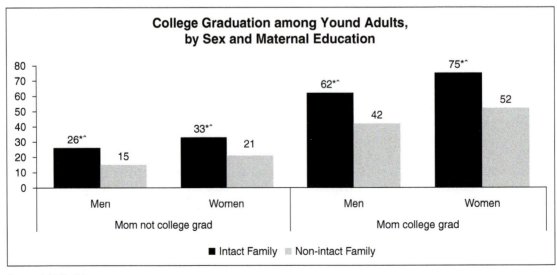

Source: Add Health

Analyses use data from Add Health Waves I and IV. Wave I was collected in 1995 when respondents were in middle and high school. Wave IV was collected in 2007 and 2008 when the participants were 24- to 32-years old. An asterisk (*) indicates a statistically significant difference (*p* < .05) between respondents who lived with both, married biological parents at Wave I compared with respondents from other family structures, controlling for respondent's age and race/ethnicity. A hat (^) indicates that there

was still a statistically significant difference when Wave I household income was added as an additional control.

The marriage bump is strongest among families where the parents didn't go to college (the left half of the graph above). Among less-educated families, the children of married parents earn about $4,000 more than their peers from nonintact families, as the next chart shows. The association between intact families and income is not significant for children of college-educated parents.

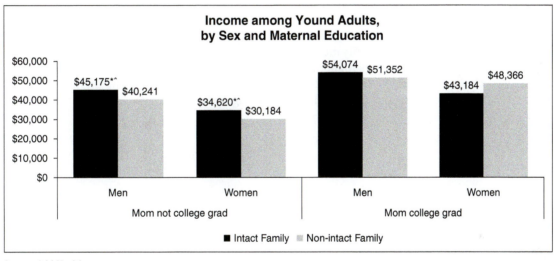

Source: Add Health

Adolescent family structure also has important implications for family formation among young adults. The next graph indicates that men and women who hail from intact families are about 40 percent less likely to father or bear a

child outside of wedlock. This is important because nonmarital childbearing reduces your odds of successfully getting and staying married down the road, maximizing your income, and of providing a stable home to your children.

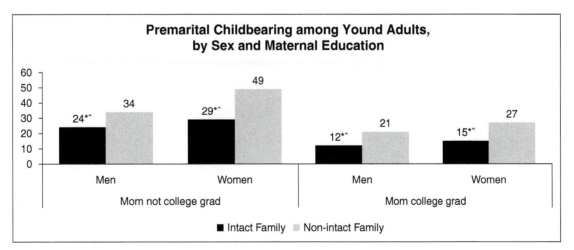

Source: Add Health

Marriage might even have economic benefits at the citywide level. A recent study from Harvard and UC-Berkeley found that the most important predictor of economic mobility was the low share of single moms in a community. Mobility for poor kids was highest in the Salt Lake City metro area, which also happens to have one of the lowest rates of single motherhood of any major metro area in the country.

The idea that marriages have such strong spillover effects strikes some as a spurious correlation. But there is evidence of a causal relationship, too. MIT economist John Gruber, studying the effect of divorce on later incomes, found that adults "exposed to unilateral divorce regulations as children are less well educated, have lower family incomes, marry earlier but separate more often, and have higher odds of suicide." Indiana psychologist Brian D'Onofrio, relying on a study of twins, also found that young adults from divorced homes did worse than their cousins from intact homes (the cousins had parents who were twins) when it came to substance abuse and behavioral problems.

The intact, two-parent family seems to be particularly important for children hailing from less privileged homes and a powerful force for economic mobility when it's the family norm at the community level. Policy makers who feel more comfortable talking about metrics than marriages need to understand that marriage could be one of the most important metrics.

W. BRADFORD WILCOX is the director of the National Marriage Project at the University of Virginia and a senior fellow at the Institute for Family Studies. He is the coauthor of Soul Mates: Religion, Sex, Love, and Marriage Among African Americans and Latinos.

Nancy Pina    **NO**

3 Ways Your Unhappy Marriage May Be Hurting Your Kids

We're often warned about the detrimental effects divorce can have on children: It can make them insecure, worried, or harm their ability to have a successful marriage later on in life. But do you really believe all that? Relationship expert and marriage and relationship coach Nancy Pina is looking at things from the flip side. Here are three reasons a divorce may just be the healthiest thing for all of you.

1. Your Relationship Will Be Your Child's "Norm" in Love

This is the most important reason a couple should not stay together if they have reached an understanding that reconciliation is impossible—and have exhausted every avenue to work through their challenges. By staying together under those conditions, modeling emotionally healthy love is impossible. The dysfunctional behavior displayed toward each other will be your children's pattern in love as they become adults. In other words, they will attract and have the highest chemistry with those who remind them of your relationship.

In unhappy marriages, the lack of positive displays of marital love is very toxic and fills the home with stress and tension. The children may be too young to know what is wrong, but they will sense all is not well. Unfortunately, when parents tell children everything is OK when it is not, kids eventually stop trusting their instincts. There is also the strong possibility that your children will fear commitment as adults, and vow never to have the type of relationship you do with your spouse. They can end up attracting a string of short-term relationships, which they sabotage when anyone gets too close and they feel too vulnerable.

2. The Facade Will Break You, Emotionally and Spiritually

Putting up an armor of denial creates pretense and that takes a great deal of energy to maintain. You may have told yourself that you are capable of living a lie for the number of years it takes for your children to grow up and then your life can begin. What you have not factored into the equation is the stress—physically, mentally, and spiritually—that will happen during those years. When your children turn 18, there is no guarantee that a divorce will not affect them just as much as it would now.

The just below the surface anger you experience from living in a loveless marriage needs an outlet. Generally, that rage will be directed at situations that do not call for such an outburst. You end up taking out those feelings of hopelessness and isolation on those you love most.

3. Inner Peace Is Impossible

If you stay in a loveless marriage, you will not be able to show emotionally healthy love to your children without receiving nurturance yourself. You cannot continually run on an empty emotional tank year after year.

Staying together for the kids denies yourself chance of working through relational issues and closes the door on the possibility of finding real love. If there is no peace in your heart—if you are living a lie to family and friends alike—you will suffer more from staying in the marriage and cutting off your authenticity than anything you would experience through a divorce.

Nancy Pina is a highly recognized author, relationship coach, and speaker. She is dedicated to helping individuals attract emotionally healthy relationships through her practical, Christian-based advice.

EXPLORING THE ISSUE

Does Marriage Impact the Well-being of Children?

Critical Thinking and Reflection

1. Happy and healthy marriages are believed to improve the well-being of children. How would you describe a marriage that is happy and healthy? What are important components of happiness and health that you believe should be emphasized in marriage, and how do you believe they impact children?
2. Marriage alone may not be enough of a protective factor to maintain the well-being of children. What are some of the negative dynamics within a marriage that might be detrimental to children? And, how would you suggest that families protect against them?
3. One aspect of well-being, financial stability, is related to marriage. Discuss the connection between these two concepts.

Is There Common Ground?

Society has undergone substantial changes with regard to perceptions about marriage in the past few decades. As evidenced by the content of television shows and movies, the emphasis on married parents raising children has diminished somewhat, and now, we have popular examples of divorced or single-parent households and children who are happy and well adjusted. It is a slow change, but we are able to see the change if we pay attention.

However, despite the greater acceptance of nonmarried parents raising children, there are still many people who believe that children are going to be better off if their parents are married. Parents who are struggling with their marriage report that they want to stay married for the sake of their children, because they believe the children will benefit from their sticking it out and would struggle too much if they did divorce. What is the right direction for parents to take? Should marriage be a qualifier for

determining the well-being of children? Or, is well-being too complicated of an issue to be connected with any one particular effect?

Additional Resources

American College of Pediatricians. Marriage and the Family. Retrieved on April 11, 2011, from www.acpeds.org/Marriage-and-the-Family.html

This website discusses some of the benefits of married families on children.

For Your Marriage. Why Married Parents Are Important for Children. Retrieved on April 11, 2011, from http://foryourmarriage.org/married-parents-are- important-for-children/

This website, put out by the Conference of Catholic Bishops, discusses information about how marriage can be important for children.

Internet References . . .

KidsHealth—Living with a Single Parent. Retrieved on April 11, 2011

This website is written for kids who live with single parents. It contains advice and suggestions for this type of living arrangement.

http://kidshealth.org/kid/feeling/home_family/single_parents.html

Single Parent Families—The Effects on Children. Retrieved on April 11, 2011

This website discusses some of the effects that children can experience when living in a single parent home.

http://family.jrank.org/pages/1577/Single-Parent-Families-Effects-on-Children.html

Selected, Edited, and with Issue Framing Material by:
Kourtney T. Vaillancourt, *New Mexico State University*

ISSUE

Do Children Who Are Homeschooled Have a Limited View of Society?

YES: Coalition for Responsible Home Education, from "Homeschooling and Socialization," *Coalition for Responsible Home Education* (2017)

NO: Brian D. Ray, from "Research Facts on Homeschooling," *Education Resources Information Center* (2015)

Learning Outcomes
After reading this issue, you will be able to: • Describe some of the reasons that parents may choose homeschooling for their children.   • Identify challenges that homeschooled children face as a result of their educational situation.   • Identify some of the benefits that children who are homeschooled can experience.

ISSUE SUMMARY

YES: The Coalition for Responsible Home Education describes how some families who home school fail to provide for the socialization needs of their children.

NO: Brian D. Ray lists some of the documents positive outcomes for homeschooled children, include a discussion about their socialization.

Home schooling was the accepted method of education in the United States until the 1850s. At that time, it was replaced by public schooling, but home schools made a comeback in the 1970's. Home schools are now legal in every state in the nation and more than two million children are home-schooled every year. According to the National Center for Education Statistics (NCES), students are considered homeschooled if their parents report them as being schooled at home instead of at a public or private school for at least part of their education and if their part-time enrollment in public or private schools does not exceed 25 hours a week. Homeschooling advocates feel that this definition does not accurately account for the true number of homeschooled children.

Parents choose to home school their children for many reasons. Some parents disagree with the values presented in public as well as private schools. They also site disagreements with specific curricula or teaching methods used by schools. Parents who favor homeschooling believe public schools do not promote self-discipline and self-motivation or provide an environment in which each child's particular talents might flourish.

According to the NCES, in 2003, the most frequently cited factor for home-schooling was parents' concern about the environment of other schools including safety, drugs, or negative peer pressure. Eighty-five percent of homeschooled students were being homeschooled, in part, because of this concern. The other two most often cited reasons for homeschooling were to provide religious or moral instruction (72 percent) and a general dissatisfaction with academic instruction at other schools (68 percent). When asked about the most important reason for the decision to homeschool, parents cited providing moral or religious instruction (33 percent) and concern about the environment of traditional schools (30 percent).

Homeschooling advocates defend their cause by pointing at the better test scores of children schooled at home. They also point to the growing problems of violence, bullying, and drug abuse in the public and private school systems. Opponents argue that homeschooled children lose vital social support and contact by being removed from the school environment. They feel that this loss of social interaction outweighs any positive academic effects.

Some educators fear that homeschooling may be harmful to a child's overall development. Children schooled at home may not have the opportunity to develop and interact with their peer group and miss learning social skills. Another common concern is that home-school teachers may not have the appropriate skills, training, education, and knowledge to teach children effectively.

Unfortunately, reliable research on this matter is hard to obtain. Homeschooling advocates point out that those who school their children at home are often resentful of their taxes being used on a school system they do not use. Advocates theorize that homeschooling parents are likely to underreport information about homeschooling.

States have differing definitions and standards of accountability for homeschoolers resulting in a lack of consistent nationwide statistics. In Florida, families can homeschool but must directly report to their school district on an annual basis. One very popular method of avoiding these responsibilities is to enroll the student in a specially established "Cover School." The family has now legally enrolled their child in a private school and has no reporting requirements to the state. In California, there are "homeschool charter schools" which get funds from the state to take responsibility for the children's education. They enroll students and provide distance education that is usually done at home. These are just two examples of different types of homeschooling. With these complexities, it is difficult to gather reliable and accurate data on children schooled at home.

As you read the following selections, think about the following questions: Do you agree that children learn important civic lessons in school? Do you believe that parents have the right to educate their children in whatever way they choose? Who has the greater interest, the state or the parents? Read the following selections and decide for yourself if children who are homeschooled have a limited view of society.

YES ↲

Homeschooling and Socialization

One of the most common questions homeschool graduates and homeschooled children face is that of socialization. In order to address this question, it is important to first understand what is meant by the term "socialization." Socialization refers to social interaction but it also refers to understanding and learning to navigate a society's social norms and rules of behavior. Most scholars view peer interaction, which generally centers on the school, as a critical component of this kind of socialization. However, many homeschool parents and leaders argue that the socialization children receive in school is unnatural and actually harmful, and that socialization is best gained through life experiences that center around the family, and should include interactions with those in a variety of age groups.

We know from both research and anecdotal data that homeschooled children can be well socialized, both in terms of learning the social norms of society and in terms of social interaction. Many homeschooled children have large social networks and active social calendars. These homeschoolers are involved in field trips, play dates, ballet or gymnastic classes, group sports, music lessons, homeschool co-ops, and even community college courses or dual enrollment courses in the local public schools, and generally integrate into the university or workplace without a hitch. However, not all homeschooled children are involved in such a wide array of social activities and some do not receive the level of socialization they need. These homeschooled children crave a greater degree of social interaction, and for some, their opportunities for social interaction are so limited that they develop social phobias or experience extreme social awkwardness. These homeschoolers may be involved in only a few social activities, and the level of social interaction these activities provide may not be adequate for their personal and social development.

How is it that homeschooling offers opportunities for healthy social development and interaction for some children but not for others? Because, quite simply, every homeschool family—and every homeschooled child—is

different. What is true for one homeschooling family may be false for another. In other words, the fact that a given homeschooled child is thriving socially and is involved in numerous activities says nothing about the experience of a homeschooled child living down the road, who may only have a few limited social outlets. Children who are homeschooled because they were bullied in school may find homeschooling an extremely positive social experience, while children who are homeschooled by parents who carefully control and limit their social lives and activities may find homeschooling socially crippling. Similarly, even with the same number of activities and social outlets, an introverted child may find homeschooling a perfect social experience while an extroverted child may feel lonely and stunted.

Researcher Brian Ray found that the homeschooled children in a 1997 study he conducted were involved in an average of 5.2 activities each week, including field trips, Sunday school, Bible club, group sports, music classes, volunteer work, and more. However, Ray also found that a full 13 percent of homeschoolers in his sample did not play with people outside of their families, suggesting that at least some homeschooled children are more socially isolated than homeschool advocates may like to admit. While Ray's study relied on volunteer participants rather than a random sample and the social opportunities available to homeschooled students have only increased in the last two decades, his findings suggest that it would be wrong to assume that every homeschooled child is involved in a large number of social activities outside of the home.

Over the past three decades, studies of homeschooled students conducted using researcher observation, various surveys designed to measure social skills, and interviews with homeschool graduates have almost universally found that homeschooled students score either as well as or better than their conventionally schooled peers in a range of social measures. However, these studies have major limitations. First, there are sampling issues. Many of these studies use extremely small sample sizes and all use volunteer participants who are likely not representative of the homeschooling population as a whole. Second, most studies rely on parents' and students' self reporting, and the pressure homeschoolers often feel to "prove" that socialization is not a problem may affect the results. As researcher Milton Gaither has pointed out, "across several studies homeschooling parents consistently rate their children higher than do parents of conventionally schooled children, though the children themselves don't rate themselves much differently at all." Finally, many of these studies have been conducted by homeschool advocates, which may bias the results.

Further, these studies actually include a fair amount of nuance. They have consistently found that homeschooled students have fewer friends and a significantly lower amount of social interaction with peers. Many researchers, especially homeschool advocates, have interpreted these results positively, arguing that homeschooled students are less peer-dependent and therefore more socially mature. However, homeschooled students in some studies have reported loneliness and a greater degree of social isolation. Further, one study of homeschooled teens and homeschool graduates found that those who had fewer social opportunities while being homeschooled expressed a less favorable attitude toward their homeschool experiences than did those who had a greater number of social opportunities, suggesting that the degree of social interaction available to homeschooled children is vitally important to the quality of their homeschool experience (Sekkes, 2004).

We have only one survey of homeschool graduates that uses a randomly selected sample, and that is the Cardus Education Survey (2011). This survey, which compared and contrasted the educational experiences of adults aged 24 to 39 who grew up in religious homes, found that homeschool graduates were significantly more likely to report "lack of clarity of goals and sense of direction" and "feelings of helplessness in dealing with life's problems" than conventionally schooled graduates. These findings back up anecdotal reports by some homeschool graduates of childhood and teenage depression, loneliness, social phobias, and a sense of cultural alienation. While the Cardus participants were randomly selected, it looked only at young adults who were raised in religious homes, and it would therefore be unwise to generalize its findings to homeschooling writ large. Further, the Cardus study focuses on the experiences of homeschool graduates who are now adults, meaning that its findings may apply more to homeschooling ten or twenty years ago than to homeschooling today. Still, the Cardus study suggests that there may be more to the story than the more positive

findings of many studies of socialization conducted over the past thirty years.

In the end, we know that homeschooled children can be well socialized in terms of both peer interaction and learning cultural norms. Many homeschooled children are involved in a wide range of activities outside of the home and maintain active social calendars. However, we also know that homeschooled children are not always well socialized. Ensuring that homeschooled children have adequate social interaction can be a lot of work for homeschooling parents, and not all do it well. Some homeschooled children are lonely and crave a greater degree of social interaction. Others may not experience loneliness but may be socially awkward when placed in certain social situations because they have never learned how to act around their peers. Finally, homeschooled children who grow up in certain homeschooling subcultures may socialize widely but only in a homogenous group, and may experience a feeling of cultural alienation when they graduate and move into the wider world. In other words, socialization can be done well in a homeschooling context, but it is something that takes time, attention, and planning.

Sources

Gaither, Milton, "Homeschooling and Socialization Revisited," International Center for Home Education Research Reviews, July 19, 2013.

Kelly, Anita E., "Pioneers on the Home Front: An Exploratory Study of Early Homeschoolers in Hawai'i" (Ph.D. diss., University of Hawai'i, 2008), pp. 25–32.

Kunzman, Robert, and Milton Gaither, "Homeschooling: A Comprehensive Survey of the Research," Other Education: The Journal of Educational Alternatives, 2 (no. 1, 2013), pp. 19–23.

Medlin, Richard G., "Homeschooling and the Question of Socialization Revisited," in Peabody Journal of Education 88, no. 3 (2013): 284–297.

Ray, Brian, "Home Schooling Achievement" (HSLDA, 2001).

COALITION FOR RESPONSIBLE HOME EDUCATION advocates for quality home education. They provide information and conduct research because they believe quality information and solid research promote good homeschooling.

Brian D. Ray

**NO**

Research Facts on Homeschooling

General Facts and Trends

- Homeschooling—that is, parent-led home-based education—is an age-old traditional educational practice that a decade ago appeared to be cutting-edge and "alternative" but is now bordering on "mainstream" in the United States. It may be the fastest-growing form of education in the United States. Home-based education has also been growing around the world in many other nations (e.g., Australia, Canada, France, Hungary, Japan, Kenya, Russia, Mexico, South Korea, Thailand, and the United Kingdom).
- There are about 2.2 million home-educated students in the United States. There were an estimated 1.73 to 2.35 million children (in grades K to 12) home educated during the spring of 2010 in the United States (Ray, 2011). It appears the homeschool population is continuing to grow (at an estimated 2 percent to 8 percent per annum over the past few years).
- Families engaged in home-based education are not dependent on public, tax-funded resources for their children's education. The finances associated with their homeschooling likely represent over $24 billion that American taxpayers do not have to spend, annually, since these children are not in public schools.
- Homeschooling is quickly growing in popularity among minorities. About 15 percent of homeschool families are non-white/non-Hispanic (i.e., not white/Anglo).
- A demographically wide variety of people homeschool—these are atheists, Christians, and Mormons; conservatives, libertarians, and liberals; low-, middle-, and high-income families; black, Hispanic, and white; parents with PhDs, GEDs, and no high-school diplomas.

Reasons for Home Educating

- Most parents and youth decide to homeschool for more than one reason.
- The most common reasons given for homeschooling are the following:

- customize or individualize the curriculum and learning environment for each child,
- accomplish more academically than in schools,
- use pedagogical approaches other than those typical in institutional schools,
- enhance family relationships between children and parents and among siblings,
- provide guided and reasoned social interactions with youthful peers and adults,
- provide a safer environment for children and youth, because of physical violence, drugs and alcohol, psychological abuse, racism, and improper and unhealthy sexuality associated with institutional schools, and
- teach and impart a particular set of values, beliefs, and worldview to children and youth.

Academic Performance

- The home-educated typically score 15 to 30 percentile points above public-school students on standardized academic achievement tests. (The public school average is the 50th percentile; scores range from 1 to 99.)
- Homeschool students score above average on achievement tests regardless of their parents' level of formal education or their family's household income.
- Whether homeschool parents were ever certified teachers is not related to their children's academic achievement.
- Degree of state control and regulation of homeschooling is not related to academic achievement.
- Home-educated students typically score above average on the SAT and ACT tests that colleges consider for admissions.
- Homeschool students are increasingly being actively recruited by colleges.

Social, Emotional, and Psychological Development

- The home-educated are doing well, typically above average, on measures of social, emotional, and psychological development. Research measures

Ray, Brian D., "Research Facts on Homeschooling," National Home Education Research Institute, March 23, 2016. Used by permission of the National Home Education Research Institute.

include peer interaction, self-concept, leadership skills, family cohesion, participation in community service, and self-esteem.

- Homeschool students are regularly engaged in social and educational activities outside their homes and with people other than their nuclear-family members. They are commonly involved in activities such as field trips, scouting, 4-H, political drives, church ministry, sports teams, and community volunteer work.

Gender Differences in Children and Youth Respected?

- One researcher finds that homeschooling gives young people an unusual chance to ask questions such as, "Who am I?" and "What do I really want?," and through the process of such asking and gradually answering the questions home-educated girls develop the strengths and the resistance abilities that give them an unusually strong sense of self.
- Some think that boys' energetic natures and tendency to physical expression can more easily be accommodated in home-based education. Many are concerned that a highly disproportionate number of public school special-education students are boys and that boys are 2.5 times as likely as girls in public schools to be diagnosed with attention deficit hyperactivity disorder.

Success in the "Real World" of Adulthood

The research base on adults who were home educated is growing; thus far it indicates that they:

- participate in local community service more frequently than does the general population,
- vote and attend public meetings more frequently than the general population, and
- go to and succeed at college at an equal or higher rate than the general population.
- by adulthood, internalize the values and beliefs of their parents at a high rate.

General Interpretation of Research on Homeschool Success or Failure

It is possible that homeschooling causes the positive traits reported above. However, the research designs to date do not conclusively "prove" that homeschooling causes these things. At the same time, there is no empirical evidence that homeschooling causes negative things compared to institutional schooling. Future research may better answer the question of causation.

Sources

The above findings are extensively documented in one or more of the following sources, all (except one) of which are available from www.nheri.org:

- Homeschooling associated with beneficial learner and societal outcomes but educators do not promote it, Brian D. Ray, 2013, *Peabody Journal of Education, 88*(3), 324–341.
- Academic achievement and demographic traits of homeschool students: A nationwide study, Brian D. Ray, 2010, *Academic Leadership Journal*, www.academicleadership.org.
- *A Sense of Self: Listening to Homeschooled Adolescent Girls.* Susannah Sheffer, 1995.
- *Home Educated and Now Adults: Their Community and Civic Involvement, Views About Homeschooling, and Other Traits*, Brian D. Ray, 2004.
- Homeschoolers on to College: What Research Shows Us, by Brian D. Ray, *Journal of College Admission*, 2004, No. 185, 5–11.
- Homeschooling and the question of socialization revisited, Richard G. Medlin, 2013, *Peabody Journal of Education, 88*(3), 284–297.
- National Education Association. (2014). *Rankings of the States 2013 and Estimates of School Statistics 2014.* Retrieved April 10, 2014 from http://www.nea.org/assets/docs/NEA-Rankings-and-Estimates-2013-2014.pdf.
- *The Truth About Boys and Girls.* Sara Mead, 2006.
- *Worldwide Guide to Homeschooling*, Brian D. Ray, 2005.

BRIAN D. RAY, PhD, is an internationally known researcher, educator, speaker, and expert witness and serves as president of the nonprofit National Home Education Research Institute. He is a former certified teacher in public and private schools and served as a professor in the fields of science, research methods, and education at the graduate and undergraduate levels. His PhD is in science education from Oregon State University and his MS is in zoology from Ohio University. Dr. Ray has been studying the homeschool movement for about 30 years.

EXPLORING THE ISSUE

Do Children Who Are Homeschooled Have a Limited View of Society?

Critical Thinking and Reflection

1. Do you believe homeschooling is a good idea or a bad one? Give three reasons for your answer from the readings.
2. What are the socialization needs of children, and how might these needs fail to be met in homeschooled children?
3. What are some of the most common reasons that parents may choose to homeschool their children? To what extent to you agree or disagree that these reasons are valid in justifying homeschooling?

Is There Common Ground?

Do children who are homeschooled have a limited view of society? Who has the greater claim on education, the state or the parents? Is a tolerant population the best thing for the state? Do you agree that it is a good thing for children to be exposed to a range of ideas? Do you agree that parents have the right and the duty to educate their children as they see fit? With an ever-increasing homeschooling population, society will continue to face this issue. The challenge is answering these questions while taking the best interest of students into consideration. It is obvious that a one-size-fits all approach to education is not the best way to go; therefore, finding some middle ground is very important in this debate.

Additional Resources

About.com Homeschooling. Retrieved on April 13, 2011, from http://homeschooling.about.com/cs/supportgroups/a/hsingusa.htm

This website provides legal information, organizations, support groups, community events, and online resources about homeschooling for each state.

A to Z Homeschool Curriculum, Laws, Programs, Social Networks. Retrieved on April 13, 2011, from http://homeschooling.gomilpitas.com/

This website is a comprehensive guide to curriculum, laws, and so forth for homeschooling.

Internet References . . .

Homeschool Central. Retrieved on April 13, 2011

This website provides resources for families who homeschool their children.

www.homeschoolcentral.com/

Public Schools vs. Home Schools. Retrieved on April 13, 2011

This website discusses the pros and cons of homeschooling versus public school.

www.allaboutparenting.org/public-schools-vs-homeschool-faq.htm

Selected, Edited, and with Issue Framing Material by:
Kourtney T. Vaillancourt, *New Mexico State University*

ISSUE

Is Television Viewing Responsible for the Rise in Childhood Obesity?

YES: **Samantha Olson**, from "Childhood Obesity Risk Rises Up To 60% When Kids Watch 1 Hour of TV," *Medical Daily* (2015)

NO: **Danielle Teutsch**, from "Study Busts Myths of TV's Link to Childhood Obesity," *The Sun Herald* (2005)

Learning Outcomes

After reading this issue, you will be able to:

- Summarize each author's stance on the reasons for the increase in childhood obesity.
- Decide which of the author's positions you feel is the largest contributor to the increase in childhood obesity and give supporting reasons for your answer.
- Demonstrate an understanding of food items that are identified as unhealthy and contributing to obesity in children as well as the types of ads that are believed to influence unhealthy eating habits.

ISSUE SUMMARY

YES: Samantha Olson describes the correlation between television watching and childhood obesity rates.

NO: Danielle Teutsch argues that it is socioeconomic status, not specifically television viewing, that contributes to childhood obesity rates.

The rise in childhood obesity is considered an epidemic because the rates of childhood overweight have grown so rapidly in such a short amount of time. According to the Centers for Disease Control and Prevention, National Center for Health Statistics, since 1980 the proportion of overweight children has more than doubled. The rate for teens has tripled since 1980. Currently, 10 percent of 2- to 5-year-olds are overweight, and 15 percent of 6- to 19-year-olds are overweight. The numbers go up to 20 percent for 2- to 5-year-old children, and 30 percent for 6- to 19-year-old children when you add in those at risk for being overweight. Children of color are at greater risk with 4 of 10 Mexican-American and African-American children being overweight.

Childhood obesity is the term used to describe the problem in the population while individual children are generally referred to as being overweight. Overweight and at risk for being overweight are terms used to define children whose height and weight fall within a certain range on a chart referred to as the body mass index (BMI). The BMI measures the ratio of weight to height. BMI measures for children are age- and gender-specific because children's body fat varies with age and gender. A child's BMI is plotted on a growth curve that reflects that child's age and gender. This plotting yields a value, BMI for age, that provides a consistent measure across age groups. Percentile scores indicate how a particular child compares with other children of the same age and gender. The Centers for Disease Control classifies children above the 95th percentile for their age and gender as overweight. Children are considered at risk for being overweight if they fall between the 85th and 95th percentile for age and gender. Healthy children have a BMI of 6 to 85 percent, and underweight children have a BMI of less than 5 percent.

Why is the rise in childhood obesity considered such a problem? Along with being overweight comes a host of physical and mental health problems such as diabetes, high blood pressure, depression, and poor body image. The health-care costs for these medical conditions are exorbitant, not to mention the reduced quality of life for the children. The probability that overweight children will become overweight adults is 50 percent; thus, these health-care issues may follow the child into adulthood. The subsequent reduced productivity levels of adults, whose overweight condition follows them into adulthood, have economic and social implications. Instead of contributing to society and the economy, individuals may be relying on these institutions to take care of them.

A review of the extensive literature that has been emerging on childhood obesity shows there are a multitude of reasons cited for the epidemic. Almost every American institution has been blamed as being responsible for the increase in children's weight. Grocery stores, schools, communities, families, restaurants, fast food, media, and the economy have had a role in making children overweight. Specifically, grocery stores are accused of stocking high-fat, high-calorie foods; the cost of healthy foods such as fruits and milk are more than processed snack foods and sodas. Schools house vending machines full of foods with little nutritive value and loads of calories; often school officials hesitate to get rid of the offending machines because they depend on them for revenue to purchase needed school supplies. There has been a reduction in the amount of hours and level of intensity of physical education classes in the schools, thus children do not get a chance to burn off calories in school the way they have in the past. Other institutions have encouraged overeating while discouraging physical activity. Communities and neighborhoods do not lend themselves to exercise with few sidewalks for walking and few parks in which to play.

The work/family dilemma of too little time shows up in family schedules that are hectic and leave little time for family meals together. Eating together as a family has been associated with reducing child weight. Parents may be contributing to childhood obesity by providing too much and the wrong type of food as well as not encouraging more physical activity of their children or themselves.

There is an overwhelming amount of media available to encourage sedentary behavior. Watching television (TV), surfing the web, and playing video games create an environment that discourages physical activity. Interestingly enough, research studies show that when children reduce time watching TV, physical exercise time does not necessarily increase; the children may replace this TV time with other sedentary activities like reading, talking on the phone, or playing board games.

Although there are many factors that contribute to childhood obesity, will the concern for reducing childhood weight turn into an obsession with weight and lead to other types of problems? Already there is a concern among educators that more eating disorders such as anorexia or bulimia will emerge. In addition, there may be more of a tendency for overweight children to be discriminated against and develop a poor body image, which can ultimately lead to mental illness and depression.

As you read the following selections, consider carefully the reasons that they each identify for the rise in childhood obesity. Which arguments fit most closely with your own perceptions? Is there research that particular stands out to you as important in understanding this complicated issue?

YES ↵

Samantha Olson

Childhood Obesity Risk Rises Up To 60% When Kids Watch 1 Hour of TV

Television (TV) can be a form of entertainment used as an educational tool, but children bathing in the screen's light for too long could be gaining excessive weight as a result. An alarming link between childhood obesity and TV was presented at the Pediatric Academic Societies annual meeting in San Diego, leading researchers to recommend a parental restriction on the remote control.

"Children who watch one to two hours of TV a day, as opposed to those who watch less, are more likely to be overweight and obese at kindergarten and first grade," the study's lead author, Dr. Mark DeBoer, associate professor of pediatrics a t the University of Virginia, said in a press release. "An hour is not that much time. In that sense, I was surprised."

Researchers analyzed data from 11,113 kindergartners collected from parents between the 2011 to 2012 school year. The study was conducted by the National Center for Education Statistics to sort out what lifestyle factors affected a child's educational performance, which included the number of hours a child watched TV, used the computer, along with their height and weight. A year later, researchers followed up with 10,853 parents and found children who watched just one hour of TV a day were 50 to 60 percent more likely to be overweight and 58 to 73 percent more likely to be obese, compared to kids who watched less than an hour.

If kids watched more than one hour of TV daily, they were 39 percent more likely to become overweight and 86 percent more likely to become obese by the time they hit first grade. In the last 30 years, childhood obesity has more than doubled in children and quadrupled in adolescence, according to the Centers for Disease Control and Prevention. Obese kids and teens are more likely to develop cardiovascular disease, high cholesterol, high blood pressure, joint problems, sleep apnea, and social stigmatization and poor self-esteem.

The health dangers don't scare off parents of ⊠ of infants and toddlers watching an average of two hours of TV a day, according to Kids Health. This doesn't meet anywhere near the American Academy of Pediatrics's recommendation to keep any child under two-years-old from watching TV and kids older than two from watching no more than one to two hours of "quality programming." Instead, the average child between the ages of two- to five-years-old is spending 32 hours a week in front of the TV.

Constant daily TV watching typically requires a sedentary lifestyle, and a lack of physical activity is the leading cause of obesity coupled with a couch-friendly bowl of unhealthy salty, sugary, and fatty foods. DeBoer says, "Given overwhelming evidence connecting the amount of time TV viewing and unhealthy weight, pediatricians and parents should attempt to restrict childhood TV viewing."

Source: DeBoer M, Peck T, and Scharf R. Viewing as Little as 1 Hour of Television Daily Is Associated with Higher Weight Status in Kindergarten: The Early Longitudinal Study. *Pediatric Academic Societies Annual Meeting.* 2015.

SAMANTHA OLSON is a Long Island native, beach bum, and runner with a passion for health. She earned her BA in Professional Writing with a Business Administration minor at King's College and her MS in Journalism at Stony Brook University. Her graduate work focused on nutrition and exercise science and continues to cover public health and wellness for women and children.

Danielle Teutsch  **NO**

Study Busts Myth of TV's Link to Childhood Obesity

Television (TV) and computer games are not to blame for children playing less sport, contrary to popular belief, a major Australian study has found.

Rather, family stability is far more important in determining whether kids are active or not.

The new research by the Australian Bureau of Statistics shows that children who played sport or danced also watched between 10 and 20 hours a week of TV and played an average of seven hours a week of computer games.

The Internet was not a problem either as children were even more likely to be active if they had access to a computer at home.

The growing tendency for children to clock up hours of screen time indoors instead of running around outside has been heavily blamed for the nation's epidemic of childhood obesity.

But study author Mike Stratton said the ABS research showed there was no reason children couldn't spend time using electronic media, as long as they balanced it with physical activity.

"This study is a challenge for a lot of people. It's a bit of a mythbuster," he said.

"There's no doubt that screen-based activities do compete for a child's time. But if you want to look at the reasons why they are really not participating [in sport], it's more to do with socioeconomics."

The single biggest factor influencing a child's lack of involvement in sport was having unemployed parents, the study showed.

This was followed by having parents born in a non–English-speaking country and having low socioeconomic status.

Children were more likely to play sport if they were in a higher socioeconomic bracket, if they were involved in cultural activities such as music, singing, and drama and if both their parents were employed.

The amount of time spent watching TV or computer games was either not significant or only slightly influenced rates of sporting activity.

Mr. Stratton, who presented the results at the Australian Social Policy Conference last week, said the results suggested family stability might be the key factor that separated active from inactive children.

"When a family has a regular income there is security, and that family can settle into a routine," he said.

"It means mum or dad can take the kids to Saturday morning, or Wednesday evening sport."

Mr Stratton said the cost of club fees, uniforms, equipment, and dance lessons might also dissuade low-income parents from enrolling their children in activities.

He said the move to incorporate sport into after-school care was the best way of ensuring all children got a fair chance to be active.

This year, the Australian Sports Commission began its Active After-school Communities Program to address the problem of childhood obesity after research found half of children aged five to 14 spent more time in front of a screen than in the classroom.

DANIELLE TEUTSCH is the National Lifestyle Editor for Fairfax Media.

Teutsch, Danielle, "Study Busts Myth of TV's Link to Childhood Obesity," *The Sun Herald*, July 24, 2005. Used with permission.

EXPLORING THE ISSUE

Is Television Viewing Responsible for the Rise in Childhood Obesity?

Critical Thinking and Reflection

1. Briefly describe each side of the issue of childhood obesity according to the authors. Give examples of supporting research provided in the readings for each perspective.
2. What is your opinion on each side of the childhood obesity issue? Do you think television viewing is the primary contributing factor or is it something else entirely? Or, do you believe that it is a combination of several things that work together to cause childhood obesity? Why?
3. What types of lifestyles are described as factors in childhood obesity?
4. Briefly describe how SES has been associated with childhood obesity.

Is There Common Ground?

Authors of numerous research reports and surveys, which have appeared in the popular press as well as professional journal articles, agree that there is an increase in the rate of childhood obesity in the United States, where the debate begins is over the reasons for this obesity epidemic.

It is evident that television viewing and SES are both contributing factors to the rates of childhood obesity. The debate, however, remains as to which is the most influential and what can be done to curb the increasing rates. A balanced perspective would include many variables in explaining childhood obesity, including other factors such as parental influence, community access to exercise and nutritious food, economic cost of nutritious food, neighborhood safety, and education.

Additional Resources

Kids Health: How TV Affects Your Child. (2008). Retrieved on May 27, 2011, from http://kidshealth .org/parent/positive/family/tv_affects_child.html#

This website provides information regarding television viewing and how it affects children. It addresses different factors associated with television viewing such as the amount of time spent watching television, negative exposures such as

violence, sexual content, and drugs that may be viewed, the effects of commercials and how too much television is associated with obesity in children. The website also provides pointers for encouraging healthy television viewing with your child.

Medical Advices: The Greatest Wealth Is Health. (2010). Retrieved on May 24, 2011, from www .medicaladvices.net/Child_Health/rising-child-hoodobesity-and-vending-machines-a14.html

This Web page addresses nutritional factors regarding vending machine food choices and how it is difficult for the schools to turn down the unhealthy food and drink choices with the financial gains they are offered from the companies. The Web page also addresses encouraging healthy eating at home.

National Center for Chronic Disease Prevention and Health: Promotion Division of Adolescent and School Health. (2010). Retrieved on May 24, 2011, from www.cdc.gov/heatlhyyouth/obesity/

This website provides some basic facts regarding childhood obesity and addresses school involvement. An article on the website explains body mass index (BMI) and national and local school-based programs that are intended to monitor BMI.

Internet References . . .

Childhood Obesity

http://www.mayoclinic.org/diseases-conditions/
childhood-obesity/home/ovc-20268886

Childhood Obesity Facts

https://www.cdc.gov/healthyschools/obesity/facts.htm

Childhood Overweight

http://www.obesity.org/obesity/resources/facts-
about-obesity/childhood-overweight

Selected, Edited, and with Issue Framing Material by:
Kourtney T. Vaillancourt, *New Mexico State University*

ISSUE

Should We Reconsider the Use of the HPV Vaccination for Girls in Later Childhood?

YES: **Shantanu Nundy**, from "Reevaluating the HPV Vaccine," *Psychology Today* (2011)

NO: **David Robert Grimes**, from "We Know It's Effective. So Why Is There Opposition to the HPV Vaccine?" *The Guardian* (2016)

Learning Outcomes

After reading this issue, you will be able to:

- Describe what the HPV vaccine is and what purpose vaccinating all young girls would serve.
- Understand each perspective regarding this issue.
- Decide where you stand on this issue and give supporting evidence.

ISSUE SUMMARY

YES: Shantanu Nundy identifies some of the cons of using the HPV vaccine that should be considered when deciding whether or not to continue advocating for its use.

NO: David Grimes addresses on concern that parents have about the HPV vaccine, which he attributes more to squeamishness about sex than opposition of the vaccine.

The human papillomavirus (HPV) vaccination may be one of the greatest health advances for women in the past several decades. In two studies by the Centers for Disease Control (CDC), the vaccine was 100 percent effective in preventing precancerous lesions and genital warts. In the second study, it was 98 percent effective in protecting against precancerous cervical lesions. Because Gardasil prevents the human papillomavirus from infecting sexually active women, the CDC recommends that females obtain the vaccination prior to becoming sexually active. They suggest being inoculated at ages 11 to 12. However, girls as young as 9 can get the vaccination, and those aged 13 to 26 are still advised to receive the vaccine even though it is not as effective if sexual activity has already begun. Since the CDC has added Gardasil to the recommended childhood vaccination schedule, several states are currently considering whether to make the vaccine mandatory for public school attendance.

Advocates for the vaccine promote universal vaccination and support laws to mandate vaccination as a prerequisite to attending school. A recent CDC study found that nearly 25 percent of women aged 14 to 59 and 49 percent of women aged 20 to 24 currently have HPV. HPV is very prevalent not only in the United States but in less industrialized countries as well. In places where Pap tests are not as readily available, there is greater prevalence of cervical cancer. In order to minimize the spread of HPV, advocates for the vaccination believe young girls across the globe should be inoculated prior to any sexual activity. To prevent deaths from measles and Polio, vaccinations for these diseases had to reach the universal level. Advocates for the HPV vaccine hope the same should happen for Gardasil.

Opponents believe vaccination should be a personal choice for parents to make for their children. Mandating inoculation would further erode parents' rights to raise their children as they see fit. Other opponents are fearful that having the vaccination may actually encourage girls to engage in premarital sex because they would not be fearful of contracting HPV. Still others prefer having regular Pap screenings, which they believe are preferable in detecting HPV, because the long-term effects of the vaccine are still unknown. They argue that the virus is not transmitted through casual contact. Consequently, the vaccination should not be universally mandated. They do not believe all girls need to be vaccinated that young. Another argument states most cases of cervical cancer in the United States come from women who do not regularly receive Pap tests. Opponents also say the vaccine is expensive and contend that the women who can afford the HPV vaccine are not the women who need it because they are annually getting Pap tests, which detect the HPV virus.

The following selections convey points for and against universal use of the HPV vaccine. Are viruses that are transmitted through casual contact more easily approved and subsequently mandated by federal law? Is sexual contact such a controversial issue that it affects the judgment of policy makers and parents? Think about these questions as you read the next two articles arguing for and against making the vaccination for HPV mandatory for young girls.

YES

Shantanu Nundy

Reevaluating the HPV Vaccine

Is the HPV Vaccine Worth It?

The human papillomavirus (HPV) vaccine has been a huge success story for the scientific, medical, and public health communities. Over the past two decades, we have gone from identifying that cervical cancer is caused by infection with the HPV virus to the development of a vaccine against certain HPV types to the widespread use and acceptance of the vaccine. This progression from basic science to clinical research to public health has occurred at a remarkable pace and set a new standard for medical discovery.

However, a number of recent articles have questioned whether we have been too quick to adopt the HPV vaccine and whether the benefits of vaccination have been oversold. In this blog article, we review some of the evidence and weigh the pros and cons of vaccination in two groups of women.

First Some Background

- Cervical cancer was once the leading cause of cancer death in women in the United States. Since the advent of cervical cancer screening (e.g., Pap smears), deaths from cervical cancer have dropped 70 percent. Still 12,000 women are diagnosed with cervical cancer each year in the United States and 4,000 women die from the disease.
- Cervical cancer is caused by the HPV virus. There are over 100 types of HPV, only a subset of which causes cervical cancer (called high-risk types).
- HPV is transmitted through sexual intercourse. It is estimated that 70 percent of adults have been infected by HPV at some point in their lives. It infects both men and women.
- The vast majority of HPV infections resolve on their own without any symptoms or complications. We do not fully understand why the infection resolves in most cases and not others.

- The HPV vaccine protects against infection with four HPV types—16, 18, 31, and 33. HPV 16 and 18 are high-risk types and are associated with 70 percent of cervical cancers. The vaccine is made by Merck and is marketed as Gardasil.
- The current Centers for Disease Control recommendations are to routinely vaccinate girls ages 11 to 12 and to vaccinate girls and women ages 13 to 26 who have not yet been vaccinated. Women who receive the vaccine are advised to continue routine screening for cervical cancer (e.g. Pap smears).

. . .

Putting All This Information Together Let's Look at Risks and Benefits of HPV Vaccination for Two Types of Women

Women with Access to Medical Care and Routine Pap Smears

Benefits

- no decrease in cervical cancer or death from cervical cancer (as discussed above, cervical cancer is rare in women who get regular Pap smears);
- no decrease in Pap smears (regardless of vaccination, women are advised to undergo routine cervical cancer screening);
- potential reduction in follow up testing and invasive procedures (Pap smears may be less likely to be abnormal due to lower rates of HPV 16 and 18).

Risks

- pain at injection site, fainting, and unknown risk of serious side effects;
- cost (in women without insurance the vaccine costs $100–$150 per dose times three doses).

Nundy, Shantanu, "Reevaluating the HPV Vaccine," *Psychology Today*, January 9, 2011. Used with permission of the author.

Conclusion

The benefits and risks of HPV vaccination are uncertain. Some women may look at the balance of benefits and risks and decide to get vaccinated, while others may look at the same information and decide that the benefits of vaccination are not worth the risks.

Women with Limited Access to Medical Care

Benefits

- potential decrease in cervical cancer and death from cervical cancer.

Risks

- pain at injection site, fainting, and unknown risk of serious side effects;
- cost (in women without insurance the vaccine costs $100–$150 per dose times three doses).

Conclusion

In women with limited access to medical care, the balance of benefits and risks is more in favor of vaccination, although a great deal of uncertainty remains.

Here Are Some of the Dangers of Our Current HPV Vaccine Strategy

- *We only have so many resources.* Even if vaccination does prevent cervical cancer and even if the side effects are minor, we have to wonder if vaccinating women who already are at low-risk of cervical cancer because of access to effective screening is a wise use of limited resources.
- *We are still missing high-risk groups.* Pre-HPV vaccine, cervical cancer predominantly affected marginalized, low-income women. Today, post-HPV vaccine, because we are primarily vaccinating women who already have access to health care or who can afford to pay for it out-of-pocket, the women who are most in need of vaccination and are most likely to benefit from it still face the same risk of cervical cancer.
- *We may stop researching the HPV vaccine.* The development and widespread acceptance of the HPV vaccine is in many ways the end of a long journey from basic science to translational research to public health. But in other ways, it's just the beginning. There are many unanswered questions about the HPV vaccine including: (a) does the vaccine ultimately prevent cervical cancer and death? (b) how long does immunity last and will booster doses be required? and (c) what are risks of vaccination? The fact that we are already administering the HPV vaccine should not deter us from answering these critical questions.

Final Thoughts

Despite limited evidence, I still support the HPV vaccine. If I were a woman, I would opt for vaccination, and as a physician, I generally counsel women to get vaccinated. My concern here is that the benefits and risks of vaccination have been overstated and that the decision to get vaccinated is not as obvious as Merck would have us believe. For most women, vaccination will not significantly alter their risk of cervical cancer. At the same time, the risks of vaccine administration are not well known. The decision then becomes a personal choice—one that requires a well-grounded understanding of what the vaccine is and what the vaccine isn't.

***

Shantanu Nundy is the director of the Human Diagnosis Project.

David Robert Grimes   NO

We Know It's Effective. So Why Is There Opposition to the HPV Vaccine?

Over 90 percent of cervical cancers are caused by HPV. But squeamishness about sex and unsupported safety fears are threatening vaccination programmes.

Human papillomavirus (HPV) has long haunted humankind; almost all sexually active adults carry some of HPV's 170 strains. And although many of these are harmless, among the myriad mutants there are those whose effects are anything but benign: subtypes 6 and 11 can lead to genital warts; subtypes 16 and 18 (amongst others) can lead to cervical, vulvar, vaginal, penile, anal, and oral cancers. This is not some mere hypothetical risk—over 90 percent of cervical cancers are caused by HPV, a cancer which claimed the lives of 270,000 women in 2012 alone.

Luckily, the HPV vaccine Gardasil is extraordinarily effective at preventing infection, being at least 99 percent effective against the four most odious subtypes (6, 11, 16, and 18) in young women. Yet despite this, it has been the subject of dogged opposition—in the United States, vaccination rates have stagnated far below the optimum levels for protection, while a number of legal challenges against the vaccine have been mounted across Europe. But why is this the case?

Broadly speaking, opposition can be separated into two distinct categories, the first of which expresses itself as moral concern. There is a sizable contingent who find the idea that their children will eventually have normal sexual urges disquieting, with some physicians also voicing opposition on moral grounds. Moral opposition to HPV vaccination is clearest in America, primarily voiced by religious conservatives, whose arguments pivot around sex rather than efficacy, advocating abstinence in lieu of vaccination. A major concern appears to be that without the fear of genital warts or cervical cancer, young people will become more promiscuous, and that the HPV vaccine therefore in effect encourages behaviour they deem immoral.

This slightly twisted assumption is flatly contradicted by the data—it operates on a strange, moralistic "consequences of sex" principle, a mantra that abstinence trumps pragmatism. Yet evidence to date clearly indicates that abstinence programmes simply don't work, and that teens subjected to this approach begin sexual activity at the same stage as their peers—worse again, teens educated in such ways tend to have more pregnancies than those receiving conventional sex education.

More damningly, the assumption that vaccination is a passport to wanton sexual abandon doesn't stand up to scrutiny—teenagers receiving the HPV vaccine tend to be far more aware of sexual health than their unvaccinated peers, and fully cogniscent of the fact that the vaccine is no panacea to sexual infections. Studies on sexual activity in vaccinated and unvaccinated teen cohorts show quite clearly that sexual activity is not elevated in the vaccinated group.

The second category of opposition is rooted in safety fears. Like all clinical compounds, Gardasil has been extensively tested for years, constantly monitored for potential adverse effects. By all measures it has been found to be a safe and effective intervention. The complication rate is extremely low, with the most common reactions being irritation at the site of injection, and fainting post injection - precisely the minor temporary reactions seen with any shot. The safety and the efficacy of the vaccine has been reaffirmed by numerous independent investigations, including a 2015 report based on data from over a million individuals which concluded the vaccine had a favourable safety profile.

Despite this, ominous reports of "vaccine-damage" still circulate. Some of this is based on simple misunderstandings, but a significant proportion is down to the success antivaccine campaigners have in sharing their claims online and across social media. In particular, claims that the HPV vaccine causes thrombosis and chronic fatigue are common, but have been comprehensively debunked. Antivaccine sites also perpetuate the falsehood that Gardasil has been banned in Japan.

Despite the paucity of evidence for damaging effects from Gardasil, there have been a number of legal challenges mounted against it, most recently in December 2015 by Fiona Kirby, who is being supported by Irish group Reactions and Effects of Gardasil Resulting in Extreme Trauma (Regret). Kirby alleges that her daughter suffered "horrendous" adverse effects after being given the vaccine, and Regret claim that upwards of 140 girls are suffering severe non-specific reactions to the vaccination, from fainting spells to fits. The group's attempt to obtain an injunction for a withdrawal of Gardasil made it to the Irish High Court, and although it was refused, the movement shows no signs of abating—if anything, they have received an incredibly sympathetic media airing.

In one respect, this is understandable: the cases are emotive, even if all evidence suggests Regret are misguided in their attempt to blame the vaccine. Their assertions are simply not supported by the copious amount of clinical evidence, nor have these trends been seen in the upwards of 200 million doses of Gardasil given worldwide to date. Given the sheer volume of teens who have received the vaccine, it is a statistical certainty that some will develop a physical or psychosomatic illness after inoculation. While this makes for an arresting anecdote, the implicit assumption that the temporal sequence is anything other than coincidental is comprehensively debunked by the scientific and statistical evidence against it.

While sensitivity by media organisations is laudable, is it completely irresponsible journalism to suspend all critical faculties when reporting on vaccines. Sadly, scaremongering anecdotes without scientific evidence all too frequently masquerade unchallenged as public interest stories, and the Gardasil controversy is no exception. In December, Irish broadcaster TV3 ran an investigation, featuring Regret's assertions prominently. These claims were frequently presented uncritically, giving these tired myths a new audience of worried parents. Such was the response to the show that the Health Service Executive had to issue a statement on it to address the panic it induced. Those of us in science outreach were left in the unenviable position

of having to counter an emotive narrative in an attempt to neutralise some of the damage done by such vapid reporting.

Such skewed coverage also triggers a chorus of populist politicians to chime in with equally vacuous additions. Indeed, so predictable is this phenomena that I've written about it before for this paper. In Ireland, a familiar list of opposition politicians from Sinn Fein to independents have regurgitated the claims verbatim, and speakers from Regret have even been invited to address the Irish parliament. One TD (member of the Irish parliament), seemingly unfamiliar with the old adage about prevention being better than cure, even questioned why there was a need for a vaccine when we have smear tests for cancer. Whether this is borne of genuine ignorance or cynical vote chasing we can only speculate, but it risks adding to the public perception there is some genuine debate over the safety and efficacy of the vaccine when this is resoundingly not the case.

The case for the safety of the HPV vaccine is buttressed by swathes of clinical evidence and years of data, whereas the opposing side is comprised of anecdotes, emotive appeals and easily debunked assertions. It a complete failure of journalism to present them as equally valid opposing views, a glaring error known as false balance. It is also irresponsible: we need only cast our minds back to the damage done by baseless scare stories "reported" about the MMR vaccine to be reminded of this fact. This propensity to sensationalism over informed reporting is one that crops up with each new or rehashed panic story. Despite the complicity of media outlets in spreading poorly researched or misleading stories, blame for this seems to be curiously evanescent.

Despite all the sound and fury from religious conservatives, antivaccine campaigners and clueless broadcasters, the unassailable crux of the matter is that the HPV vaccine has the potential to save lives. We cannot afford to let squeamishness about sex dictate our health policy, nor should we allow falsehoods to cloud our judgment. The lives of countless young men and women count on us being guided by evidence rather than rhetoric.

Dr. David Robert Grimes is a physicist and cancer researcher at Oxford University. He is a regular Irish Times columnist and blogger.

EXPLORING THE ISSUE

Should We Reconsider the Use of the HPV Vaccination for Girls in Later Childhood?

Critical Thinking and Reflection

1. What population receives the HPV vaccine? What is the purpose of this vaccine and what does it protect against?
2. Briefly describe each author's perspective about making the HPV vaccine mandatory for young and adolescent girls.
3. What is your opinion about this issue? Should the government be able to make a vaccination that is so relatively new mandatory without knowing its long-term effects?

Is There Common Ground?

Some opponents of the HPV vaccination are believed to be squeamish about sex, and therefore resistant to a vaccine that deals with a sexually transmitted disease. Likewise, moral concerns and objections are often cited when Gardasil is opposed, and instead abstinence is suggested as the right choice. However, there is research that supports the notion that abstinence-only is not an effective strategy in preventing sexually transmitted diseases like HPV. What do you think, do you believe that moral objections should be honored when it comes to determining which vaccinations a child receives and which they do not?

Opponents of mandating the HPV vaccination argue that we may have been too quick to act on implementing the vaccine for children, because there are still mitigating factors to be considered. There is an argument that pap smears are more effective in identifying and preventing cervical cancer than Gardasil. Additionally, the argument is made that we are still missing high-risk groups who do not receive the vaccine, and that we may be vaccinating young girls who are not at risk to begin with. Do these arguments lend support to a stopping of the current vaccination schedule for young women? Surely, the debate on this is nowhere near concluded, as opponents and oppositionists continue to explore the issue and its cost versus its overall impact.

Additional Resources

Centers for Disease Control and Prevention. (2011). Human Papillomavirus. Retrieved on April 24, 2011, from www.cdc.gov/hpv/

This website provides information about HPV regarding prevention, treatment, signs and symptoms, and so forth. The website also gives information regarding being vaccinated.

Health Information and Education. (2011). Helping Parents Understand the HPV Vaccine. Retrieved on April 24, 2011, from www.healthed.org/consulting/Articles/20081216ParentsUnderstandHPVVaccine.htm

This website addresses questions that parents may have regarding the HPV vaccine. It provides information about the safety of the vaccine as well as other issues that parents may have with deciding whether or not to have their daughters vaccinated.

The American Congress of Obstetricians and Gynecologists. (2010). Ob-Gyns Recommend HPV Vaccination for Young Girls: Adolescents and Young Women May Also Benefit. Retrieved April 24, 2011, from www.acog.org/from_home/publications/press_releases/nr08-23-10-3.cfm.

This article gives supporting evidence for vaccinating girls as young as 11 or 12 for HPV as well as some guidelines that parents should know with regard to the vaccine.

Internet References . . .

Centers for Disease Control and Prevention

www.cdc.gov/vaccines/vpd-vac/hpv/vac-faqs.htm

PBS

www.pbs.org/newshour/bb/health/jan-june13/hpv_06-20.html

Unit 4

UNIT

Adolescence

*M*any people use the term teenage years to describe adolescence. This is the period of time from ages 13 through 19. During this period of development, the child typically begins puberty, and there are dramatic physical changes that occur as the child becomes a young adult. Much less obvious than the physical changes are the cognitive and emotional changes in children at this stage of development.

In early adolescence, the child is increasingly able to think on an abstract level. Adolescents also undertake the daunting process of identity development, defining who they are. This final section considers some of the key issues related to decisions about values and sexuality that teens make as they move through adolescence.

Selected, Edited, and with Issue Framing Material by:
Kourtney T. Vaillancourt, *New Mexico State University*

Are Male Teens More Aggressive Than Female Teens?

YES: Lori Rose Centi, from "Teenage Boys: From Sweet Sons to Narcissistic Teens," *The Washington Times* (2012)

NO: Frances McClelland Institute, from "Aggression Among Teens: Dispelling Myths About Boys and Girls," *Research Link* (2009)

Learning Outcomes
After reading this issue, you should be able to:
• Describe the overall findings from each article that either support or do not support gender differences with regard to aggression in teens.
• Decide for yourself if the research presented is compelling enough to help you decide which side of the issue you are on.

ISSUE SUMMARY

YES: Lori Rose Centi addresses the differences in male and female brain development, and how gray and white matter in the brain can impact adolescent behaviors. She also discusses other brain changes that may contribute to males being more impulsive and less careful than their female peers.

NO: The Frances McClelland Institute shares a fact sheet which dispels "myths" about the differences in male and female teens. It reports on a meta-analysis of 148 studies and the resulting major findings. Different types of aggression are defined and discussed.

Research on aggression and adolescents suggests that aggressive acts are neither uncommon nor restricted to a certain demographic. School bullying and aggression cut across all economic, cultural, ethnic, and gender boundaries. The reported rates of bullying and aggression for the United States suggest that a significant number of adolescents have either been a victim of school aggression or have bullied others themselves. This is a concern because aggression is associated with a host of behavioral, social, and emotional adjustment difficulties.

In order to answer the question "Are male teens more aggressive than female teens?" it is important to understand what we mean by "aggression." Social scientists define aggression as behavior intended to hurt, harm, or injure

another person. However, research has demonstrated that children engage in a variety of forms of aggressive behavior. The most important distinction for classification purposes is whether aggression is physical or relational in form.

Physical, or direct, aggression consists of behaviors that harm another through damage to one's physical well-being. Physical aggression among adolescents has received considerable attention from researchers. Some have argued that there is a general tendency for physical violence to worsen over time, with behaviors like minor aggression giving way to more serious behaviors, including assault and robbery. Other research has shown that, among boys, early physical aggression predicts an elevated risk of physical violence in adolescence as well as nonviolent forms of delinquency.

Relational, or indirect, aggression includes behaviors that harm others through damage to relationships or feelings of friendship, acceptance, or social inclusion. Existing evidence suggests that relational aggression, like physical aggression, can result in emotional harm to victims. Outcomes include a range of psychosocial problems including lower social and emotional adjustment, poorer relationships with peers, and more loneliness. An added concern among some researchers who study relational aggression is the potential for retaliatory violence by those who have been victimized. Research has shown that a majority of females use relational aggression to secure their social status and maintain social harmony.

In general, convention states that males tend to employ more physical aggression, while females are more likely to use relational aggression. However, recent research suggests that it is not always appropriate to categorize aggression types by gender. Several studies have found that male and female teens appear to use a complex combination of both physical and relational aggression.

In addition to the aggression issue, be mindful of the age group on which these selections focus. Adolescence is a time of physical, developmental, social, and emotional change. Adolescents often feel out of control and overwhelmed by daily living. Remember when you were a teenager? Were you ever a victim or perpetrator of physical or relational aggression? Who were more aggressive, males or females? Which one of these views best reflects your experiences?

The question remains: Are male teens more aggressive than female teens? As you read the following two selections, keep in mind the different types of aggression.

YES ↵

Lori Rose Centi

Teenage Boys: From Sweet Sons to Narcissistic Teens

HUNTINGDON, PA—January 8, 2012—Teenage boys can be an enigma to their mothers, who are often perplexed by the way their sweet young boys have seemingly morphed overnight into moody, narcissistic young teenagers.

A plethora of images fill a mother's mind when considering her teenage son and his behaviors. Some of the images may be of laughing and talking together, enjoying time outdoors, or pleasant family time playing cards or board games. Other images may not be as positive.

These less than positive experiences, involving some recalcitrant behaviors, uncharacteristic outbursts, demands for more freedom and fewer rules, may not completely be the teen's fault. In other words, his growing, developing brain may be at "fault," but he as a person is not completely to blame. Recent research conducted on the development of the male and female brains, beginning in infancy and often continuing to age 20, have corroborated many psychiatrists' (and parents') previous assertions with physiological findings.

These findings may help parents to not only understand their teenage sons better, but also to advocate for the enhancement of education geared toward reaching both sexes more effectively. It may also make parents of teens feel less frustration and more empathy for their growing, often misunderstood, sons.

Many friends and colleagues have expressed confusion about the differences between their male and female children, especially during the teen years. Comments, such as "He is so immature compared to her," and "He seems to be unable to control his anger at times, while she just cries," are commonly heard in the parenting realm. Now, at least, the research has revealed valid, solid reasons for the sometimes churlish, impulsive behavior exhibited by our male offspring.

"Adolescence is a period of rapid changes. Between the ages of 12 and 17, for example, a parent ages as much as 20 years." Author unknown.

The National Institute of Health released a report on "Male/Female Difference Offers Insight into Brain Development" stating "there are gender differences in the trajectory of gray matter maturation in adolescent girls and boys that may have lasting effects on the brain." Male adolescent brains have more gray matter than female brains. Gray matter is sometimes called "thinking matter."

However, developing female brains have more white matter, responsible for connecting various parts of the brain than their male counterparts. So, in spite of this seeming "advantage," boys are actually at a disadvantage because the information acquired usually cannot be fully processed due to the inability of their brains to make adequate connections.

Perhaps the actual physiology of male and female teens' brains is the most revealing aspect of the studies. The cortex, which contains both gray and white matter, is the part of the brain responsible for thinking, perceiving, and processing language. More specifically, the prefrontal cortex, a portion of the brain right behind the forehead, is one of the last areas of the brain to mature in males. This part of the brain is necessary for "good judgment, controlling impulses, solving problems, setting goals, organizing and planning, and other skills that are essential to adults," according to "The Amazing Adolescent Brain," compiled by Dr. Linda Burgess Chamberlain, Ph.D., MPH.

In addition to the physiology of the brain, a teen's gender and hormones affect his or her developing brain in myriad ways. It may also help you to understand why your son spends hours on video games that involve more violence than you and your husband have allowed him to see in his short lifetime. In addition, you may now understand why your son grunts or mutters incomprehensible words while his fingers rapidly press buttons on his game controller.

Hormones contribute greatly to the differences in male and female brain development. The hippocampus, which helps to move newly acquired information into long-term storage in the brain, responds to the primary female hormone, estrogen. As a result, the hippocampus grows and matures much faster in teenage girls than in teenage boys. This cerebral advantage allows girls to do better in social settings and causes them to show emotions more freely than boys.

Conversely, the amygdala and the hypothalamus are affected by male sex hormones and, consequently, grow larger in teenage males. Both of these parts of the brain are involved in responding to frightening and/or dangerous situations. These brain functions are exhibited by boys' greater enjoyment of physically challenging sports and being more aggressive in some settings than females.

It also may, in part, explain their need for excitement, whether literal or virtual. (Hence, those video games.) Researchers also contend that this aspect of brain development makes males less able to sit still for long periods of time. For that reason, males often learn better while moving around in a learning environment.

The greatest difference between the male and female adolescent brains, however, appears to be the delayed development of the prefrontal cortex.

Mark Weist, Ph.D., professor of psychology at the University of South Carolina and the father of three boys and two girls, concurs that male brains take longer to mature.

"Compared to teenage girls, teenage males have less developed brain functions in the frontal lobe region, associated with more impulsive behavior and less careful processing of information."

Unfortunately for males, brain development often continues into the early to mid-20s. This puts them at a higher risk for engaging in dangerous, superfluous behaviors that could cause them to make poor decisions. If drug or alcohol use is involved, brain development may also be adversely affected.

So how can parents and/or family members assist teenage boys though this difficult time? One thing that experts recommend is encouraging your son, family member, etc., to become actively involved in athletic endeavors, artistic activities (such as theatrical productions),

and outdoor recreation. Being physically and mentally involved in activities that allow teens to move around while learning is especially beneficial to males. These kinds of activities are also both mentally and physically stimulating, so they aid in the development of the brain as well.

In addition, parents should also remember that because the prefrontal cortex is still developing in male teens, it is wise to give them simple instructions, rather than overwhelming them with information. Also, the information should be given in a step-by-step fashion.

It is helpful to give your teenager a planner to help him organize his homework and extra-curricular activities. Ask him to be responsible and listen to the teacher or coach's instructions, then write the instructions in the planner. This will help to reinforce the information that has been conveyed to him.

Neuroscientists stress that both male and female teenagers are often sleep-deprived due to a biological tendency to become drowsy later at night than adults. Sleep deprivation can exacerbate teenagers' tendencies to make poor decisions or to act impulsively. Parents should encourage their teenagers to get a minimum of nine hours of sleep per night. Getting extra sleep on weekends is also beneficial.

During the teen years of rapid growth and change, teenagers need family togetherness and ties that only you can give him or her. Family dinners and discussions are as important to his development into a person of good character and responsibility as any facet of his educational process.

"Even as kids reach adolescence, they need more than ever for us to watch over them. Adolescence is not about letting go. It's about hanging on during a very bumpy ride," according to Ron Taffel, renowned child development expert.

LORI ROSE CENTI is a writer and a teacher on the postsecondary level.

Frances McClelland Institute

 **NO**

Aggression Among Teens: Dispelling Myths About Boys and Girls

A new study dispels the popular belief that girls are more likely than boys to hurt other children through gossip, rumor, and social rejection. While boys do tend to hit, push, and call their peers names more than girls do, they are just as likely as girls to hurt other kids socially.

Background

Why study aggression in children and adolescents? Such behaviors are associated with maladjustment—that is, difficulties coping with problems and social relationships. For over 100 years, scientists have studied children who physically and verbally attack other kids, what we now call "direct" aggression. Since most people previously thought that physical attacks were typical of boys, researchers often left girls out of their studies. In addition, in the last 20 years, girls have been linked with social or "indirect" aggression—that is, they hurt other girls through talking badly about them and keeping them out of their social group. Over time, a belief has grown that social aggression is a female form of aggression. But new evidence shows that boys hurt their peers socially, too. . . .

The study also dispelled another myth, that girls tend not to be physically aggressive. This myth may exist because public opinion is more likely to approve the use of direct aggression by boys than by girls. But even though boys use direct aggression more than girls, girls are directly aggressive, too.

Implications

- We need to study direct and social aggression, but not because one is a male form and the other female. Both forms of aggression affect both genders, and boys and girls who engage in aggression are equally likely to experience maladjustment.
- To understand whether aggression causes poor adjustment, or vice versa, we need to do longitudinal studies. We must look at aggressive kids over time to see which condition—aggression or maladjustment—comes before the other.
- People who work with aggressive children can look for signs of delinquent behavior, attention problems, depression, or anxiety. Indirectly aggressive

THIS RESEARCH BRIEF SUMMARIZES THE FOLLOWING REPORT:

Card, N. A., Stucky, B. D., Sawalani, G. M., & Little, T. D. (2008). Direct and indirect aggression during childhood and adolescence: A meta-analytic review of gender differences, intercorrelations, and relations to maladjustment. *Child Development, 79,* 1185–1229.

SUGGESTED CITATION FOR THIS RESEARCH LINK:

Van Campen, K. S., & Card, N. A. (2009). Aggression Among Teens: Dispelling Myths About Boys and Girls (Frances McClelland Institute for Children, Youth, and Families Research Link Vol. 1, No. 2). Tucson, AZ: The University of Arizona.

children are as much at risk for problems as directly aggressive children.
- Researchers can look at the source of perceptions of aggression. Do they arise in adult or children's minds?

About the Study

A recent meta-analysis examined 148 studies that consisted of almost 74,000 children. The goal of the meta-analysis, which examined direct and social forms of aggression, was to understand three things:

1. Are direct and social aggression more common among boys or among girls, and how large are these gender differences?
2. To what extent are children who are directly aggressive also socially aggressive, and vice versa?
3. How much does aggressive behavior explain the likelihood that a child will suffer from problems such as depression or delinquency? . . .

Finding 1

Boys tend to engage in hitting and punching more than girls, but girls do physically hurt others to a moderate degree. For example:

- Imagine a school with 100 boys and 100 girls, and 100 children are directly aggressive and 100 are not.
- Of these 100 aggressive children, about 65 would be boys and 35 would be girls.
- So even though direct aggression is nearly twice as common among boys than girls, there are still a lot of girls who use direct aggression.

Boys and girls are equally likely to use social aggression. For example:

- Imagine again a school with 100 boys and 100 girls, and 100 children are indirectly aggressive and 100 are not.
- Of these 100 indirectly aggressive children, about 51 would be girls and 49 would be boys.
- The amount of difference in social aggression between boys and girls is so small that it is not meaningful.

Finding 2

Physically and socially aggressive behaviors tend to be used together. For example:

- Imagine again a school of 200 children and that 100 of them are directly aggressive and 100 are indirectly aggressive.
- Because there is overlap between the two forms, about 85 or 90 children use both direct and social aggression.
- But because the two forms are not perfectly overlapping, there is a large number—about 20 to 30—who use only one form or the other.
- So, although most aggressive children will use both types, some will only use one form or the other.

Finding 3

Both direct and social aggression are related to behavioral problems, but to different types. For example:

- There is a *strong* link between direct aggression and problems we can see in a child. That is, children who hit and punch tend to misbehave and act impulsively more so than children who gossip and hurt others socially.
- Directly aggressive children are also more likely to have poor relations with their peers than other children.
- There is a *moderate* link between social aggression and problems that are harder to see. That is, children who are indirectly aggressive are more likely to suffer from depression and anxiety than other children.
- Children who use direct aggression show low prosocial behavior (e.g., helping, sharing, cooperating), while children who use social aggression show high rates of acting prosocially toward others.
- No matter which type of aggression they use, girls and boys experience poor adjustment in the same ways. This finding contradicts previous beliefs that boys who gossip and spread rumors and girls who hit and punch are especially likely to have poor adjustment.

Misperceptions of Aggression in Girls

The myth that girls tend to be more socially aggressive than boys is strong among teachers, parents, and even some researchers. These adults may set social expectations for girls early in life that are hard to shake. Recent movies and books that depict girls as mean and hurtful maintain these stereotypes. According to the meta-analysis, teachers and parents were more likely to say that girls were more socially aggressive than boys. Meanwhile, peers and research observers were likely to view boys and girls as equally socially aggressive.

> "These findings challenge the popular belief that social aggression is a female form of aggression," says Noel A. Card, assistant professor of Family Studies and Human Development at The University of Arizona and the study's lead author.

FRANCES MCCLELLAND INSTITUTE for Children, Youth, and Families serves as a catalyst for cross-disciplinary research on children, youth, and families at the University of Arizona.

EXPLORING THE ISSUE

Are Male Teens More Aggressive Than Female Teens?

Critical Thinking and Reflection

1. What evidence did each article present for whether the authors believe there are gender differences in aggressive behavior among teens?
2. Identify some limitations in each article regarding the participants, methods, and overall generalizability to the entire teen population. Given these limitations, can you think of ways to improve these studies and build on the research?

Is There Common Ground?

Both articles examined gender differences in aggression among teenage males and females. However, neither of the articles mentioned the ethnic or cultural background. Whether this was omitted for the purposes of condensing the articles or it was just left out, could this information explain some of the findings? How might ethnic or cultural background influence aggression in each gender? What about teens in rural versus urban areas?

Both sets of researchers utilized children from elementary school as part of their study, partly to examine patterns of aggression based on earlier experiences and behavior patterns at a younger age into adolescence. How might the results of their findings be different if only adolescents had been used? Although information regarding the behaviors from childhood to adolescents is important, is it possible that these behaviors may change as the adolescents move further away from their preadolescent years?

Can you think of ways in which the research presented and other research like it will contribute to school-age children (elementary through high school)? What is the significance of knowing whether gender differences exist with regards to these possible contributions of the research?

Additional Resources

Karriker-Jaffe, K. J., Foshee, V. A., Ennett, S. T., & Suchindran, C. (2008). The Development of Aggression During Adolescence: Sex Differences in Trajectories of Physical and Social Aggression Among Youth in Rural Areas. *Journal of*

Abnormal Child Psychology, 36(8), pp. 1227–1236. doi: 10.1007/s10802-008-9245-5. Retrieved on April 24, 2011, from www.ncbi.nlm.nih.gov/pmc/articles/PMC2773662/.

The authors report findings in the study that support that male teens tend to be more physically aggressive than female teens.

National Youth Violence Prevention Resource Center. (2002). Facts for Teens: Aggression. Retrieved on April 24, 2011, from http://herkimercounty.org/content/departments/View/11:field=services;/content/DepartmentServices/View/68:field=documents;/content/Documents/File/123.PDF

This website offers information about different types of aggression and explains some of the contributing factors to aggression in adolescents and how this might relate to earlier childhood.

Nichols, T. R., Graber, J. A., Brooks-Gunn, J., & Botvin, G. J. (2006). Sex Differences in Overt Aggression and Delinquency Among Urban Minority Middle School Students. *Applied Developmental Psychology*, 27, pp. 78–91. doi: 10.1016/j.appdev.2005.12.006. Retrieved on April 24, 2011, from www.med.cornell.edu/ipr/PDF/Nichols-et-al-2006-JADP.pdf

This article describes a longitudinal study that examined minority male and female adolescents' aggressive behavior with relation to precursors such as family disruption, anger, and self-control.

Internet Reference . . .

Global Post

http://everydaylife.globalpost.com/aggressive
-behavior-teenagers-2848.html

Scientific American

www.scientificamerican.com/article.cfm?id=bitch
-evolved-girls-cruel

Selected, Edited, and with Issue Framing Material by:
Kourtney T. Vaillancourt, *New Mexico State University*

ISSUE

Is the Internet Damaging Teen Brains?

YES: **Chandra Johnson**, from "Growing Up Digital: How the Internet Affects Teen Identity," *Deseret News* (2014)

NO: **Lauren Sherman**, from "Internet and the Teen Brain: What Do We Know, and What Should We Be Asking?" *Psychology in Action* (2014)

Learning Outcomes

After reading this issue, you will be able to:

- Summarize the main concerns associated with children/teens' Internet use.
- Identify some ways in which parents can help their child/teen avoid exposure to harmful Internet material.
- Decide how safe you think teen brains are when they use the Internet.

ISSUE SUMMARY

YES: Chandra Johnson describes some of the harmful effects that the Internet can have on teenagers.

NO: Lauren Sherman advocates for more research to be conducted before a firm determination is made about the impact of the Internet on adolescents.

Parents want to protect their children. When children are young, they are under parental control and easier to protect because they are physically in parents' sight. They are dependent on parents for physical needs such as food and shelter. As children get older, they are more mobile, particularly when they learn to drive. Parents of teens are usually sleep deprived because they cannot sleep until they know their teens are home safely from a night activity with their friends. But how can parents protect their children from the dangers of the Internet? Teens can be right in front of them in the house working on the computer and still be in possible danger. They don't even have to be out of the house to be exposed to dangers on the Internet such as sexual predators.

Is this true or is it an exaggeration? Although media reports suggest that children and teens are being sexually solicited on the Internet at an alarming rate, some researchers state that the incidence of sexual predators

on the Internet is grossly overstated. Media reports often quote the statistic that one in five children, aged 10 to 17, per year, are sexually solicited online. What they don't tell you is that this statistic comes from a report that defines sexual solicitation as anything from a classmate asking his girlfriend if she is a virgin to something more serious like adults asking children to meet for a sexual encounter. One is a simple question, while the other is an example of the serious problem of online predators.

Studies on Internet use and its effects report conflicting and varied results. Some studies on children's use of the Internet show that it has positive effects on academic achievement and no negative effects on social or psychological development. Other studies report children experience lasting psychological damage as a result of surfing the Web. For example, one study stated that 42 percent of Internet users aged 10 to 17 had seen online pornography in the past year, with the majority saying that they did not seek it out and were very disturbed by it. Of the more than 450 million porn Web sites, 3 percent ask for proof of age and are more than willing to show scenes that are sexually explicit.

Common Sense Media and Media Wise from the National Institute on Media and the Family list Internet safety by age and stage as well as rules on Internet safety. For children aged 2 to 6, they suggest keeping children away from the Internet, even the games. For ages 7 to 9, e-mailing is OK, but not instant messaging (IM) as it is too difficult to control. Web surfing can be done if a filter is installed. No chat rooms, online games, or downloading should be allowed for this age group. For ages 10 to 12, children begin exploring the Web much more at school,

at home, and at their friends' homes. They insist on IMing and surfing the Web for games and need to be supervised closely. Social media is inappropriate at this age. Children age 13 to 16 can e-mail, IM, surf the Web, download, and play games as long as they follow the rules of Internet safety.

In the following selections, the impact of Internet use on teen brains is debated. As you read the arguments, consider your own online use and the impact that it seems to have had on you. And, consider how a parent might feel about their child(ren) using the Internet, what should some of their concerns be and what should they not worry too much about?

YES ↵

Chandra Johnson

Growing Up Digital: How the Internet Affects Teen Identity

This is the final story in a three-part series on the ways new technology is impacting kids and teens. Read part one: How digital culture is changing the way kids play. Read part two: How digital screens are changing the way we read.

When British 14-year-old Hannah Smith turned to popular social networking site Ask.fm in July 2013, she wanted reassurance.

Stressed out from studying for exams and anxious about the return of eczema that made her feel ugly, Smith opened up about her feelings on the site, which allows users to pose questions others can respond to anonymously. The responses came in rapid succession. Anonymous posters urged Smith to cut herself and drink bleach. One even said, "Do us all a favour n kill ur self." When Smith did just that a month later, her father blamed the anonymity of Ask.fm's commenters for his daughter's death. The family demanded action against the site, and Smith's death made international headlines about the effects of cyberbullying.

What detectives found was arguably much more tragic—that Smith sent the hateful messages to herself, hoping her friends would rally in her defense.

While cases like Smith's are rare, Smith was doing what most teenagers do: seeking identity validation from friends and strangers, often via social media. As a new generation comes of age online, the Internet could be affecting how they form their identity.

Catherine Steiner-Adair, a psychologist and author of "The Big Disconnect: Protecting Childhood and Family Relationships in the Digital Age," says the kind of outside affirmation Smith sought online is a vital part of how teens form identity.

"The need for validation and confirmation that you're OK is so huge," Steiner-Adair said. "Parents often say, 'How could you go on a site where people can anonymously respond to whatever your question is: Am I cute? Am I fat?' But we're forgetting what it means to be a teenager when we say things like that."

Social media allow kids to broadcast everything while connecting them to experiences they might not have encountered a generation ago. But it also opens teens up to exponential ridicule or an amplified feeling of invisibility that can influence the perceptions they have of themselves.

According to market research data released this year from GFK, a German market research institute, the amount of time teens spend online has grown 37 percent since 2012, to about four hours a day. In a 2010 survey from the Girl Scout Research Institute, 74 percent of girls said they felt their peers used social media to "make themselves look cooler than they are," and 41 percent said that also describes them.

A 2010 study from York University found that people with lower self-esteem spent more time online and posted more "self-promotional" content to sites like Facebook.

Steiner-Adair says that while technology changed how teens seek and get feedback about identity, teen behavior is much the same.

"Kids are always looking at each other, comparing themselves to each other. The same thing that's going on in the halls is going on online," Steiner-Adair said. "The difference for teenagers today is that there's an endless supply of people to whom they can compare themselves."

Read Part One: How Digital Culture Is Changing the Way Kids Play

Online versus Real-time Identities

Experts like Steiner-Adair and Dr. David Greenfield say the fact that many teens view their online and real-time identities as identical can be a recipe for disaster.

The problem is impulse control, says Greenfield, an assistant professor of psychiatry at the University of Connecticut School of Medicine and founder of the Center for Internet and Technology Addiction. He says that because teens' brains aren't fully developed, they don't have the impulse control to understand the damage they can do online.

"This group doesn't differentiate. They see their real-time identity and their online identity as identical when in fact they're not," Greenfield said. "Along with that, there's now no delay between the urge to do something and the ability to broadcast it instantaneously. They do and say things online that they ordinarily wouldn't do because it doesn't feel real to them. But what you do in cyberspace follows you into real space."

When the online and real-time identities don't match—or when a hoard of anonymous commenters say they don't—it can get dangerous, Steiner-Adair said.

"Kids spend a lot of time crafting this identity that you hope people will respond favorably to," Steiner-Adair said. "When they feel desperate for feedback or curious in a risky way, social networking sites like Ask.fm play very much on the vulnerability of teens' and preteens' desire to not only know what people think of them but their hopes that they're seen as cool and their hunger for approval."

The Struggle to Differentiate

Technology can also make it more difficult to form an identity. There are more versions of "self" than ever before, which gives kids who may already be struggling to figure out who they are even more to juggle. In an interview with NPR, media theorist and author Douglas Rushkoff explained the feeling in a term he coined: "digiphrenia."

"'Digiphrenia' is the experience of trying to exist in more than one incarnation of yourself at the same time. There's your Twitter profile, your Facebook profile, your email inbox," Rushkoff said. "All of these sort of multiple instances of you are operating simultaneously and in parallel. And that's not a really comfortable position for most human beings."

In their effort to individualize on the Web, teens use different accounts in different ways, as researcher Katie Davis found out while co-authoring "The App Generation: How Today's Youth Navigate Identity, Intimacy and Imagination in a Digital World."

"There's this interesting dichotomy online where there's an emphasis toward identity consolidation and having this crystallized identity that is well-formed for many different audiences versus an increased opportunity to present different identities," Davis said, explaining that teens often adapt their online identities almost like creating a brand.

The focus on the external image detracts from the creation of a true identity, which Davis says takes serious meditation. "They're tailoring and promoting almost a branded 'self.' If you're all of your time projecting an identity externally, it crowds out the time you have for internal reflection."

The kind of self-promotion or expression varies depending on the network.

"If they're on Facebook, their identities are available for many different audiences to see. So that restricts how they can express themselves because they have to make sure it's OK for a wide audience," Davis said.

The natural urge to seek approval online can create a dependency on the Internet, Greenfield said. Because teens are digital natives, they have a higher likelihood for addiction. He says you can see it in the way teens handle their cellphones.

"[The phone] is so much more than a way of communicating," Greenfield said. "They would no more be out and about without a phone than they'd go without underwear. It's become part of their identity on a social and cultural level."

Davis and Gardner call it "app-dependent behavior," and while it's rare, it's also a recent development. For example, if a young person has a homework assignment, he or she might go online to get the facts, but Davis said an app-dependent person would also look for analysis of those facts to use in a book report rather than thinking about it themselves.

The same sort of app-dependency rears itself in relationships, where some people rely on talking online rather than in person. Others might depend on Facebook input to make decisions as small as which movie to see or even to resolve personal or moral dilemmas.

"Their online lives and offline lives are both real to them, and they do move fluidly between the two," Davis said. "But I think some young people who become very highly involved in an online community may have a harder time integrating that identity into the real world."

Read Part Two: How Digital Screens Are Changing the Way We Read
Digital Role Modeling

The most important tool kids have in their favor is a good parent, the experts say.

"A lot of parents think that because they (don't) understand tech, they throw up their hands. You don't have to know (exactly how technology works) to set the right kinds of limits," Steiener-Adair said.

Parents must be good digital role models, Davis said.

"Parents are very powerful models for their kids," Davis said. "They see how tied their parents are to technology. It's really not about the technology; it's really about how we use it and how dependent we are on technology."

Steiner-Adair came to a similar conclusion while researching her book when she interviewed 1,000 kids ages 4–18 about how much their parents used digital devices. She said she consistently heard from children of every single age that they often felt ignored, frustrated, sad, lonely, or mad when vying for their parents' attention or help.

"I talked to one young woman who told me, 'They just asked me about my first semester in college for two seconds and then they stopped to make a dinner reservation,'" Steiner-Adair said. "This is not a way we want our children to feel. They do need to know that their parents cherish them."

Edutopia urges parents to be sympathetic to teens' worries and questions and be familiar with which sites are popular among kids in different age groups.

To help control kids' impulses, Steiner-Adair says, first teach kids how to use the cameras on their phones appropriately rather than for humiliation. Treat devices at sleepovers the same as alcohol: Lock them up or put them out of sight. Make kids understand the power they wield with a smartphone.

"They're playing in a different sandbox. Kids are being kids with a tool that has far more powerful impact than they understand," Steiner-Adair said. "Parents are feeling understandably overwhelmed by all the challenges technology brings with it. At the same time, this is the age in which we are parenting."

CHANDRA JOHNSON is a Utah transplant who has covered the justice system, education, social services, and politics. Originally from Montana, she graduated with a BA in journalism and history from the University of Montana in 2007. After six years in Taos, New Mexico, she relocated to Utah, where she eventually joined the team at The Deseret News as an enterprise reporter. She enjoys wide-open spaces, gardening, good grammar, pottery, and long walks in the library.

Lauren Sherman

 **NO**

Internet and the Teen Brain: What Do We Know, and What Should We Be Asking?

Teenagers—and more specifically, their brains—are having something of a moment in the psychological literature and popular press. Noninvasive imaging tools like fMRI allow us to peek at adolescents' cognition in real time and to build a better understanding of the brain's developing structure. You may be familiar with research suggesting that the brain continues to mature well into the 20's and that some of the last regions to complete this maturation are involved in higher-order processes like planning for the future and inhibiting impulses. Our growing knowledge of the teen brain has important implications in a variety of domains, including legal culpability and appropriate educational practices.

And we just can't get enough of it. I could cite dozens of articles from *the New York Times, Huffington Post, Time Magazine*, and many more, but most telling, I think, is Pixar's recently released trailer for their upcoming film, "Inside Out," which literally dives into the mind of a girl on the verge of adolescence (My take: my job would be a heck of a lot simpler if Mindy Kaling and Amy Poehler would just narrate the various cognitive processes going on during my experiments. Hollywood, let's talk). The Pixar-ization of the emerging teen brain suggests that the concept is more than a meme; it's such a cultural touchstone that it has become the stuff of modern fairy tale. And why not? Teenagers are up there with witches and big bad wolves in terms of the things that keep us up at night. But why is this the case? Just what is so *scary* about teenagers?

As I see it, the adolescent experience may frighten or perplex us because it contains a central contradiction. On the one hand, some aspects of this period feel universal—the emotional highs and lows, the sudden looming reality of adulthood, the intense importance of peers' opinion. Our memories of the emotional and social component of adolescence don't fade and, in fact, a sizable body of research actually suggests that our memories in adolescence and early adulthood loom larger than those from other periods. This phenomenon is known as the reminiscence bump.

On the other hand, adolescence is a period during which we do a tremendous amount of cultural learning and thus, the individual experiences of teens throughout time and across societies vary tremendously. They vary so much that parents often have difficulty understanding the appeal of their sons' and daughters' day-to-day activities and interests, whether we're talking about current chart-topping music or the allure of selfies. In fact, teens are *so good* at absorbing (and creating) sociocultural information that some researchers have proposed that the adolescent years are a **sensitive period** for social development. If this hypothesis is true, it would mean that something about the very plasticity of our brains is uniquely tuned for social learning during the second decade of life.

And perhaps this is why we are so afraid: if the teen brain is so sensitive to the cultural landscape in which one comes of age, what does it mean that today's teens are growing up at a time in which so much of this landscape is rendered on a smartphone? Surely, our very noisy and expensive neuroimaging machines can settle this question one way or the other, right?

For all the hand wringing—and there sure has been a lot of it—very little research has actually been conducted on the subject of digital media and the adolescent brain. A recent article by University College London researcher Kate Mills reviews this limited literature. Her conclusion? We still have a lot of work to do: "There is currently no evidence to suggest that Internet use has or has not had a profound effect on brain development."

Mills is suggesting, quite rightly, that we haven't actually done much to test the effect of the Internet or digital media on the teen brain—at least, published research on this topic is very limited, although several labs around the world are beginning to consider these questions. But what are these questions, exactly? Can we test whether "the Internet has a profound effect on brain development"? Is that a sound empirical question? I would argue that it is not. Rather, the relationship between digital media and the developing adolescent brain is more complex, and involves a variety of other concerns that must first be considered. For example:

Sherman, Lauren, "Internet and the Teen Brain: What Do We Know, and What Should We Be Asking?" *Psychology in Action*, December 22, 2014. Used by permission of the author.

What Do We mean by "the Internet"?

The Internet is not a single entity. When we ask about the effect of the Internet, are we talking about social media? Overall screen time? Online video games? And *how* are teens using the Internet: to communicate? To learn new information? To avoid paying attention in class? And are we talking web sites or apps, laptops or smartphones? Digital media serves a variety of functions; even an individual tool can be used in many ways. Consider Snapchat, for example: journalists and parents worried that teens would primarily use the ephemeral photo-texting app to send one another explicit photos. Certainly, this is one way that teens (and adults!) can use the tool. But as the app became popular, I noticed teens using it in an unexpected way: to take pictures of themselves making silly faces to send to friends.

In work I've done with young college students, we discovered that friends felt more connected when they had a conversation face-to-face compare to online. However, communicating on video-chat also inspired feelings of connectedness; in fact, video chat more closely resembled in-person communication than it did text messaging in terms of the experience of bonding with a close friend. The medium made a big difference!

What Is Digital Media Replacing?

Another important question to consider is what teens would be doing during the time that they spend digitally connected. Recently, my colleague Yalda blogged about her work looking at the effects of quitting screen time cold turkey during for five days at camp She and her coauthors discovered that the participating tweens significantly improved in their ability to make judgments about others' emotions. So did the lack of screens improve their socioemotional functioning? I think it's reasonable to conclude that it was a factor. But it's also important to consider what screen-time was *replaced* by: team-building exercises, group activities, outdoor activities, and physical exercise.

So *does* online communication replace opportunities for in-person communication? Not necessarily. In Mills paper, she cites recent research suggesting that, "time spent online does not displace time spent doing other activities associated with health and well-being," including sports and clubs.

What Are the Implications If the Internet *Does* Profoundly Affect the Teen Brain?

Although the actual evidence is limited, I'm willing to bet that Internet use does affect the brains of children, teens, and adults. If we do anything long enough, our brain is affected—even if at a level that can't be measured using current imaging technology, which works in notoriously broad strokes. Does this necessarily mean it is *bad* or *dangerous* if we document long-term changes in the brain? That isn't so clear cut.

Which leads me to a final question: **Does the rise of digital technology mean the end of civilization as we know it?** In all seriousness, though, when it comes to these sorts of fears about change and the kids these days, we've been here before. As Mills notes in her article, Plato and Socrates were busy tut-tutting about the crazy youths and their new-fangled ideas about *writing stuff down*. This doesn't mean that all teens will face the coming years unscathed—some will face video game or porn addiction, or feel a tugging emptiness in their social connections. And most of them will ignore their parents at least a few times in favor of a more enticing Snapchat or the newest Kim Kardashian app update. But does neuroscience and psychology research suggest that the Internet is ruining their brains? As Mills demonstrate, the jury is still very much out. I do have a sneaking suspicion, however, that the kids are going to be all right.

Lauren Sherman is a doctoral candidate in developmental psychology at UCLA and a researcher at the Children's Digital Media Center@LA and the Ahmanson-Lovelace Brain Mapping Center. She originally hails from Philadelphia and received her BA in psychology and music from Vassar College. Lauren studies the ways that children, teens, and emerging adults interact with digital technology and social media and the ways that these interactions influence development. She also studies functional brain development during adolescence, particularly as it relates to social development. When she is not studying the ways your children text, chat, blog, and YouTube (or doing it herself!), she likes to read fiction and sing opera.

EXPLORING THE ISSUE

Is the Internet Damaging Teen Brains?

Critical Thinking and Reflection

1. What are some of the concerns with children and teens being on the Internet that were mentioned in both articles?
2. What did the authors identify as some ways in which parents can help decrease their child/teen's exposure to damaging Internet material? Can you think of other ways that parents can help to ensure their teens' safety online?
3. What is your opinion on teen brains and Internet use?

Is There Common Ground?

It is difficult to discuss the Internet without discussing safety from sexual predators and the risks that children and teens face online. As we have continued to develop into a 24/7 technology-laden society, though, we have begun to worry not only about safety from harm from outside influences, but also from the impact that Internet use has on brain development. Everyone wants to protect teens who use technology, but there is not agreement about what they need to be protected from, nor the best way to do so.

What are some of the negative influences of the Internet that you identify or hypothesize may be out there? And, what ideas do you have for helping parents to prevent this from occurring? Given the indelible nature of technology, where do we draw the line on teenage use in a balanced way?

Additional Resources

National Center for Missing and Exploited Children.

(2010). Net Smartz Workshop. Retrieved on April 29, 2011, from www.netsmartz.org/Teens

This website provides information about remaining safe online and also has videos of teens telling their own stories of becoming victims of online predators and other situations.

Teens Health. (2011). Internet Safety: Safe Surfing Tips for Teens. Retrieved on April 29, 2011, from http://kidshealth.org/teen/safety/safebasics/internet_safety.html

This website provides information for teens to help them identify information that should always be kept private as well as how to deal with encountering uncomfortable situations in chat rooms or handling cyberbullying.

Washington State Office of the Attorney General. (2008). Internet Safety. Retrieved on April 29, 2011, from www.atg.wa.gov/InternetSafety/Teens.aspx

This site provides information and tips on how to remain safe on the Internet and social networking sites. It provides some scenarios and points out common mistakes that teens make while using the Internet that can put them at risk.

Internet References . . .

Huffington Post

www.huffingtonpost.com/news/internet-safety

Microsoft Safer Online Facebook page

www.facebook.com/saferonline

Palo Alto Medical Foundation

www.pamf.org/teen/life/risktaking/internet.html

Selected, Edited, and with Issue Framing Material by:
Kourtney T. Vaillancourt, *New Mexico State University*

ISSUE

Is Cyberbullying Really a Problem?

YES: Stopbullying.gov, from "What Is Cyberbullying?" *U.S. Department of Health and Human Services* (2013)

NO: Nick Gillespie, from "Stop Panicking About Bullies," *The Wall Street Journal* (April 2012)

Learning Outcomes
After reading this issue, you should be able to:
• Describe some of the effects that bullying may have on a child or adolescent.
• Discuss the reasons why bullying has gained so much media attention in recent years.
• List some ways in which parents can intervene if their child is the victim of a bully.

ISSUE SUMMARY

YES: Stopbullying.gov defines cyberbullying and the potential effects it can have on victims. It also discusses the frequency of cyberbullying, according to recent studies.

NO: Nick Gillespie acknowledges that bullying occurs, but argues that there are other issues that parents should be more concerned about. He discusses some of the reasons he believes that people have become so sensitive to bullying, and how it may be impacting parenting strategies.

No one would deny that being bullied is a problem. For decades studies have focused on how bullying impacts both the victim and the perpetrator. Programs worldwide have worked on preventative programs to keep bullying out of schools. The I-SAFE Foundation reports that over half of all teens have been bullied online, and also over half of all teens have engaged in cyberbullying of someone else. The foundation also states that one in three young people experience threats online, 25 percent have been repeatedly bullied through cell phones and online. And, at least half of young people do not report the bullying to their parents, and only one in five reports to law enforcement.

The numbers are generally not being debated. What is being debated, however, is how serious cyberbullying actually is with regard to long-term impact on the victim. Society has a tendency to minimize threats that come from electronic sources due to the usual lack of physical danger.

Technology can provide tremendous opportunities and conveniences, and most of us would be reluctant to give it up. However, as you read the following selections, consider how technology is changing the face of bullies and the ways that victims are being impacted. Is the psychological, as opposed to physical, damage real and of great concern? Or, is it simply "harmless" and "over blown"?

YES ↵

Stopbullying.Gov

What Is Cyberbullying?

Cyberbullying is *bullying* that takes place using electronic technology. Electronic technology includes devices and equipment such as cell phones, computers, and tablets as well as communication tools including social media sites, text messages, chat, and websites.

Examples of cyberbullying include mean text messages or emails, rumors sent by email or posted on social networking sites, and embarrassing pictures, videos, websites, or fake profiles. . . .

Why Cyberbullying Is Different

Kids who are being cyberbullied are often bullied in person as well. Additionally, kids who are cyberbullied have a harder time getting away from the behavior.

- Cyberbullying can happen 24 hours a day, 7 days a week, and reach a kid even when he or she is alone. It can happen any time of the day or night.
- Cyberbullying messages and images can be posted anonymously and distributed quickly to a very wide audience. It can be difficult and sometimes impossible to trace the source.
- Deleting inappropriate or harassing messages, texts, and pictures is extremely difficult after they have been posted or sent.

Effects of Cyberbullying

Cell phones and computers themselves are not to blame for cyberbullying. Social media sites can be used for positive activities, like connecting kids with friends and family,

helping students with school, and for entertainment. But these tools can also be used to hurt other people. Whether done in person or through technology, the effects of bullying are similar.

Kids who are cyberbullied are more likely to:

- Use alcohol and drugs
- Skip school
- Experience in-person bullying
- Be unwilling to attend school
- Receive poor grades
- Have lower self-esteem
- Have more health problems

Frequency of Cyberbullying

The 2008–2009 *School Crime Supplement* (National Center for Education Statistics and Bureau of Justice Statistics) indicates that 6% of students in grades 6–12 experienced cyberbullying.

The 2011 *Youth Risk Behavior Surveillance Survey* finds that 16% of high school students (grades 9–12) were electronically bullied in the past year.

Research on cyberbullying is growing. However, because kids' technology use changes rapidly, it is difficult to design surveys that accurately capture trends. . . .

STOPBULLYING.gov is a federal government website managed by the U.S. Department of Health & Human Services designed to bring education and awareness, and provide resources to the public about the issue of bullying.

U.S. Department of Health and Human Services. From stopbullying.gov.

Nick Gillespie  **NO**

Stop Panicking About Bullies

Childhood is safer than ever before, but today's parents need to worry about something. Nick Gillespie on why busybodies and bureaucrats have zeroed in on bullying.

"When I was younger,"a remarkably self-assured, softspoken 15-year-old kid named Aaron tells the camera, "I suffered from bullying because of my lips—as you can see, they're kind of unusually large. So I would kind of get [called] 'Fish Lips'—things like that a lot—and my glasses too, I got those at an early age. That contributed. And the fact that my last name is Cheese didn't really help with the matter either. I would get [called] 'Cheeseburger,' 'Cheese Guy'—things like that, that weren't really very flattering. Just kind of making fun of my name—I'm a pretty sensitive kid, so I would have to fight back the tears when I was being called names.

It's hard not to be impressed with—and not to like— young Aaron Cheese. He is one of the kids featured in the new Cartoon Network special "Stop Bullying: Speak Up," which premiered last week and is available online. I myself am a former geekish, bespectacled child whose lips were a bit too full, and my first name (as other kids quickly discovered) rhymes with two of the most-popular slang terms for male genitalia, so I also identified with Mr. Cheese. My younger years were filled with precisely the sort of schoolyard taunts that he recounts; they led ultimately to at least one fistfight and a lot of sour moods on my part.

As the parent now of two school-age boys, I also worry that my own kids will have to deal with such ugly and destructive behavior. And I welcome the common-sense antibullying strategies relayed in "Stop Bullying": Talk to your friends, your parents and your teachers. Recognize that you're not the problem. Don't be a silent witness to bullying.

But is America really in the midst of a "bullying crisis," as so many now claim? I don't see it. I also suspect that our fears about the ubiquity of bullying are just the latest in a long line of well-intentioned yet hyperboiic alarms about how awful it is to be a kid today.

I have no interest in defending the bullies who dominate sandboxes, extort lunch money and use Twitter to taunt their classmates. But there is no growing crisis. Childhood and adolescence in America have never been less brutal. Even as the country's overprotective parents whip themselves up into a moral panic about kid-on-kid cruelty, the numbers don't point to any explosion of abuse. As for the rising wave of laws and regulations designed to combat meanness among students, they are likely to lump together minor slights with major offenses. The antibullying movement is already conflating serious cases of gay-bashing and vicious harassment with things like . . . a kid named Cheese having a tough time in grade school.

How did we get here? We live in an age of helicopter parents so pushy and overbearing that Colorado Springs banned its annual Easter-egg hunt on account of adults jumping the starter's gun and scooping up treat-filled plastic eggs on behalf of their winsome kids. The Department of Education in New York City—once known as the town too tough for Al Capone—is seeking to ban such words as "dinosaurs," "Halloween" and "dancing" from city-wide tests on the grounds that they could "evoke unpleasant emotions in the students," it was reported this week. (Leave aside for the moment that perhaps the whole point of tests is to "evoke unpleasant emotions.") . . .

Now that schools are peanut-free, latex-free, and soda-free, parents, administrators and teachers have got to worry about something. Since most kids now have access to cable TV, the Internet, unlimited talk and texting, college and a world of opportunities that was unimaginable even 20 years ago, it seems that adults have responded by becoming ever more overprotective and thin-skinned.

Kids might be fatter than they used to be, but by most standards they are safer and better-behaved than they were when I was growing up in the 1970s and '80s. Infant and adolescent mortality, accidents, sex and drug use—all are down from their levels of a few decades ago. Acceptance of homosexuality is up, especially among younger Americans. But given today's rhetoric about bullying, you could be forgiven for thinking that kids today are not simply reading and watching grim, postapocalyptic fantasies like "The Hunger Games" but actually inhabiting such terrifying terrain, a world where "Lord of the Flies" meets "Mad Max 2: The Road Warrior," presided over by Voldemort'. . . .

Which isn't to say that there aren't kids who face terrible cases of bullying. The immensely powerful and highly acclaimed documentary "Bully," whose makers hope to create a nationwide movement against the "bullying crisis," opens in selected theaters this weekend. The film follows the harrowing experiences of a handful of victims of harassment, including two who killed themselves in desperation. It is, above all, a damning indictment of ineffectual and indifferent school officials. No viewer can watch the abuse endured by kids such as Alex, a 13-year-old social misfit in Sioux City, Iowa, or Kelby, a 14-year-old lesbian in small-town Oklahoma,without feeling angry and motivated to change youth culture and the school officials who turn a blind eye.

But is bullying—which the stopbullying.gov website of the Department of Health and Human Services defines as "teasing," "name-calling," "taunting," "leaving someone out on purpose," "telling other children not to be friends with someone," "spreading rumors about someone," "hitting/kicking/pinching," "spitting" and "making mean or rude hand gestures"—really a growing problem in America?

Despite the rare and tragic cases that rightly command our attention and outrage, the data show that things are, in fact, getting better for kids. When it comes to school violence, the numbers are particularly encouraging. According to the National Center for Education Statistics, between 1995 and 2009, the percentage of students who reported "being afraid of attack or harm at school" declined to 4% from 12%. Over the same period, the victimization rate per 1,000 students declined fivefold.

When it comes to bullying numbers, long-term trends are less clear. The makers of "Bully" say that "over 13 million American kids will be bullied this year," and estimates of the percentage of students who are bullied in a given year range from 20% to 70%. NCES changed the way it tabulated bullying incidents in 2005 and cautions against using earlier data. Its biennial reports find that 28% of students ages 12–18 reported being bullied in 2005; that percentage rose to 32% in 2007, before dropping back to 28% in 2009 (the most recent year for which data are available). Such numbers strongly suggest that there is no epidemic afoot (though one wonders if the new anti-bullying laws and media campaigns might lead to more reports going forward). . . .

None of this is to be celebrated, of course, but it hardly paints a picture of contemporary American childhood as an unrestrained Hobbesian nightmare. Before more of our schools' money, time and personnel are diverted away from education in the name of this supposed crisis, we should make an effort to distinguish between the serious abuse suffered by the kids in "Bully" and the sort of lower-level harassment with which the Aaron Cheeses of the world have to deal. . . .

Our problem isn't a world where bullies are allowed to run rampant; it's a world where kids like Aaron are convinced that they are powerless victims.

Nick Gillespie is editor in chief of Reason.com and Reason.tv and the co-author of "The Declaration of Independents: How Libertarian Politics Can Fix What's Wrong with America."

EXPLORING THE ISSUE

Is Cyberbullying Really a Problem?

Critical Thinking and Reflection

1. What does cyberbullying entail and what distinguishes it from more physical acts of bullying?
2. What can parents do to help minimize their child's exposure to cyber bullying?
3. Do you believe that cyberbullying is mostly harmless, or is it a serious threat to teens today? Why?

Is There Common Ground?

No one would stand up and say that bullying, even cyberbullying, is acceptable behavior. Any time that someone is hurt by the words or threats of others, it is important to acknowledge that as unacceptable behavior. What is at issue, however, is how much impact words can actually have on someone. Even adults admit to using the Internet or their text messaging to tease, taunt, or disparage someone else. Plus, the additional anonymity that online sources provide may embolden someone who might otherwise hold their tongue to engage in mistreatment of another. Prevention is obviously important and a major focus of parental and educator efforts. However, what remains to be determined is how much of a focus should be placed on cyberbullying in comparison to more traditional forms of bullying when creating and implementing anti-bullying campaigns.

Additional Resources

Bullying Statistics. Cyber Bullying Statistics. Retrieved on May 21, 2013, from www.bullyingstatistics.org /content/cyber-bullying-statistics.html

Enough Is Enough. Internet Safety 101. Retrieved on May 21, 2013, from www.internetsafety101.org /cyberbullyingstatistics.htm

Stop Bullying. Reaching Teens Through Social Media. Retrieved on May 21, 2013, from www.stopbullying. gov/blog/2013/04/09/reaching-teens-through-social-media

Internet References . . .

Do Something

www.dosomething.org/tipsandtools/11-facts-about
-cyber-bullying

Girl's Health

www.girlshealth.gov/bullying/whatis
/cyberbully.cfm

Selected, Edited, and with Issue Framing Material by:
Kourtney T. Vaillancourt, *New Mexico State University*

ISSUE

Is Social Media Use Detrimental to Teens?

YES: Rachel Ehmke, from "How Using Social Media Affects Teenagers," *Child Mind Institute* (2017)

NO: Peg Streep, from "4 Things Teens Want and Need from Social Media," *Psychology Today* (2013)

Learning Outcomes
After reading this issue, you will be able to:
• Identify some of the reasons that social media is appealing to teenagers.
• Identify some of the concerns that have been raised about social media use by teenagers.
• Describe some protective factors that should be implemented for teenagers who use social media.

ISSUE SUMMARY

YES: Rachel Ehmke identifies several risks associated with teenage social media use.

NO: Peg Streep identifies some of the needs of teenagers that social media can fulfill.

In the past 20 years, social media has become a part of most Americans' everyday lives. It began simply enough with platforms like America Online that had "online chat forums," to ICQ (I-Seek-You) which was a direct messaging service, then proceeded to MySpace, Facebook, Twitter, Snapchat, Instagram, and will it will inevitably continue to evolve. Individuals of all ages access social media, but the platforms that they choose to use tends to vary by age, with adults feeling that they cannot keep up with the newest ones nearly as quickly as their children do. I have often heard teenagers say that once their parents and grandparents joined Facebook, it lost its appeal for them so they moved to Instagram and Snapchat, which are still considered to be for the "younger" crowd. With the technology changing so quickly, parents can often feel ill prepared to appropriately set boundaries and expectations for their children's social media use.

The Pew Research Center (http://www.pewresearch.org/) has conducted regular surveys about the use of technology among adolescents, and following are some of their most important findings:

Teens connect via mobile. Widespread and improved mobile technology means teens can access social media more easily. According to a Pew survey conducted during 2014 and 2015, 94 percent of teens who go online using a mobile device.

- **Teens use multiple social platforms.** Facebook, Instagram, and Snapchat are the most popular ⌕, and 71 percent of teens say they use more than one social media site.
- **Teens' social media use differs by gender.** Boys report going on Facebook most often ⌕; while girls are more likely than boys to use visually oriented platforms such as Tumblr, Pinterest, and Instagram.

- **Teens share a lot of their personal information.** A survey of over 600 teens from 2012 found that nearly all shared their real name and photos of themselves, and most shared their school name, birthdate, and the city or town where they lived.
- **Teens use social media for romance too.** Another 2015 Pew report—PDF on the role of technology in teen romantic relationships notes that half of teens say they've used Facebook or other social networking sites to express romantic interest in someone, and many use these sites to display their romantic relationships.

As noted by Pew, not only have social media sites become a part of everyday experiences, the means by which we access them has also been greatly developed. Handheld devices like tablets and smartphones with unlimited internet access now make it possible to be connected to our social networks without interruption. Whereas in the past we could recommend that parents place a computer in a shared room in the house so that they could see what their teens were doing, now the screens are so small and mobile that it is much harder for parents to regularly monitor what their children are up to.

With all that we know about adolescents' social media use, there is still so much that we need to learn. Before we can really adequately be able to discuss how best to manage social media use in teens, we need to understand how it impacts their life. In the first selection here, Rachel Ehmke discusses the psychological impact that social media is having on teens, to include increased levels of anxiety and lowered self-esteem. On the opposite side, Peg Streep provides a discussion about four things that teens can gain from social media use, if they use it appropriately.

YES ↵

Rachel Ehmke

How Using Social Media Affects Teenagers

Learn the impact of social media on youth. Experts say kids are growing up with more anxiety and less self-esteem.

Many parents worry about how exposure to technology might affect toddlers developmentally. We know our preschoolers are picking up new social and cognitive skills at a stunning pace, and we don't want hours spent glued to an iPad to impede that. But adolescence is an equally important period of rapid development, and too few of us are paying attention to how our teenagers' use of technology—much more intense and intimate than a 3-year-old playing with dad's iPhone—is affecting them. In fact, experts worry that the social media and text messages that have become so integral to teenage life are promoting anxiety and lowering self-esteem.

Indirect Communication

Teens are masters at keeping themselves occupied in the hours after school until way past bedtime. When they're not doing their homework (and when they are), they're online and on their phones, texting, sharing, trolling, scrolling, you name it. Of course before everyone had an Instagram account teens kept themselves busy, too, but they were more likely to do their chatting on the phone, or in person when hanging out at the mall. It may have looked like a lot of aimless hanging around, but what they were doing was experimenting, trying out skills, and succeeding and failing in tons of tiny real-time interactions that kids today are missing out on. For one thing, modern teens are learning to do most of their communication while looking at a screen, not another person.

There's no question kids are missing out on very critical social skills.

"As a species we are very highly attuned to reading social cues," says Dr. Catherine Steiner-Adair, a clinical psychologist and author of *The Big Disconnect*. "There's no question kids are missing out on very critical social skills. In a way, texting and online communicating—it's not like it creates a nonverbal learning disability, but it puts

everybody in a nonverbal disabled context, where body language, facial expression, and even the smallest kinds of vocal reactions are rendered invisible."

Lowering the Risks

Certainly, speaking indirectly creates a barrier to clear communication, but that's not all. Learning how to make friends is a major part of growing up, and friendship requires a certain amount of risk-taking. This is true for making a new friend, but it's also true for maintaining friendships. When there are problems that need to be faced—big ones or small ones—it takes courage to be honest about your feelings and then hear what the other person has to say. Learning to effectively cross these bridges is part of what makes friendship fun and exciting, and also scary. "Part of healthy self-esteem is knowing how to say what you think and feel even when you're in disagreement with other people or it feels emotionally risky," notes Dr. Steiner-Adair.

But when friendship is conducted online and through texts, kids are doing this in a context stripped of many of the most personal—and sometimes intimidating—aspects of communication. It's easier to keep your guard up when you're texting, so less is at stake. You aren't hearing or seeing the effect that your words are having on the other person. Because the conversation isn't happening in real time, each party can take more time to consider a response. No wonder kids say calling someone on the phone is "too intense"—it requires more direct communication, and if you aren't used to that it may well feel scary.

If kids aren't getting enough practice relating to people and getting their needs met in person and in real time, many of them will grow up to be adults who are anxious about our species' primary means of communication—talking. And of course social negotiations only get riskier as people get older and begin navigating romantic relationships and employment.

Cyberbullying and the Imposter Syndrome

The other big danger that comes from kids communicating more indirectly is that it has gotten easier to be cruel. "Kids text all sorts of things that you would never in a million years contemplate saying to anyone's face," says Dr. Donna Wick, a clinical and developmental psychologist who runs Mind to Mind Parent. She notes that this seems to be especially true of girls, who typically don't like to disagree with each other in "real life."

"You hope to teach them that they can disagree without jeopardizing the relationship, but what social media is teaching them to do is disagree in ways that are more extreme and do jeopardize the relationship. It's exactly what you don't want to have happen," she says. . . .

Dr. Steiner-Adair agrees that girls are particularly at risk. "Girls are socialized more to compare themselves to other people, girls in particular, to develop their identities, so it makes them more vulnerable to the downside of all this." She warns that a lack of solid self-esteem is often to blame. "We forget that relational aggression comes from insecurity and feeling awful about yourself, and wanting to put other people down so you feel better."

Peer acceptance is a big thing for adolescents, and many of them care about their image as much as a politician running for office, and to them it can feel as serious. Add to that the fact that kids today are getting actual polling data on how much people like them or their appearance via things like "likes." It's enough to turn anyone's head. Who wouldn't want to make herself look cooler if she can? So kids can spend hours pruning their online identities, trying to project an idealized image. Teenage girls sort through hundreds of photos, agonizing over which ones to post online. Boys compete for attention by trying to out-gross one other, pushing the envelope as much as they can in the already disinhibited atmosphere online. Kids gang up on each other.

Adolescents have always been doing this, but with the advent of social media, they are faced with more opportunities—and more traps—than ever before. When kids scroll through their feeds and see how great everyone seems, it only adds to the pressure. We're used to worrying about the impractical ideals that photoshopped magazine models give to our kids, but what happens with the kid next door is photoshopped, too? Even more confusing, what about when your own profile doesn't really represent the person that you feel like you are on the inside?

"Adolescence and the early twenties in particular are the years in which you are acutely aware of the contrasts between who you appear to be and who you think you are," says Dr. Wick. "It's similar to the 'imposter syndrome' in psychology. As you get older and acquire more mastery, you begin to realize that you actually are good at some things, and then you feel that gap hopefully narrow. But imagine having your deepest darkest fear be that you aren't as good as you look, and then imagine needing to look that good all the time! It's exhausting."

As Dr. Steiner-Adair explains, "Self-esteem comes from consolidating who you are." The more identities you have, and the more time you spend pretending to be someone you aren't, the harder it's going to be to feel good about yourself.

Stalking (and Being Ignored)

Another big change that has come with new technology and especially smart phones is that we are never really alone. Kids update their status, share what they're watching, listening to, and reading, and have apps that let their friends know their specific location on a map at all times. Even if a person isn't trying to keep his friends updated, he's still never out of reach of a text message. The result is that kids feel hyperconnected with each other. The conversation never needs to stop, and it feels like there's always something new happening.

"Whatever we think of the 'relationships' maintained and in some cases initiated on social media, kids never get a break from them," notes Dr. Wick. "And that, in and of itself, can produce anxiety. Everyone needs a respite from the demands of intimacy and connection; time alone to regroup, replenish and just chill out. When you don't have that, it's easy to become emotionally depleted, fertile ground for anxiety to breed."

It's also surprisingly easy to feel lonely in the middle of all that hyperconnection. For one thing, kids now know with depressing certainty when they're being ignored. We all have phones and we all respond to things pretty quickly, so when you're waiting for a response that doesn't come, the silence can be deafening. The silent treatment might be a strategic insult or just the unfortunate side effect of an online adolescent relationship that starts out intensely but then fades away.

"In the old days when a boy was going to break up with you, he had to have a conversation with you. Or at least he had to call," says Dr. Wick. "These days he might just disappear from your screen, and you never get to have the 'What did I do?' conversation." Kids are often left imagining the worst about themselves.

. . .

But even when the conversation doesn't end, being in a constant state of waiting can still provoke anxiety. We can feel ourselves being put on the back burner, we put others back there, and our very human need to communicate is effectively delegated there, too.

What Should Parents Do?

Both experts interviewed for this article agreed that the best thing parents can do to minimize the risks associated with technology is to curtail their own consumption first. It's up to parents to set a good example of what healthy computer usage looks like. Most of us check our phones or our e-mail too much, out of either real interest or nervous habit. Kids should be used to seeing our faces, not our heads bent over a screen. Establish technology-free zones in the house and technology-free hours when no one uses the phone, including mom and dad. "Don't walk in the door after work in the middle of a conversation," Dr. Steiner-Adair advises. "Don't walk in the door after work, say 'hi' quickly, and then 'just check your e-mail.' In the morning, get up a half hour earlier than your kids and check your email then. Give them your full attention until they're out the door. And neither of you should be using phones in the car to or from school because that's an important time to talk."

Not only does limiting the amount of time you spend plugged in to computers provide a healthy counterpoint to the tech-obsessed world, it also strengthens the parent–child bond and makes kids feel more secure. Kids need to know that you are available to help them with their problems, talk about their day, or give them a reality check.

"It is the mini-moments of disconnection, when parents are too focused on their own devices and screens, that dilute the parent-child relationship," Dr. Steiner-Adair warns. And when kids start turning to the Internet for help or to process whatever happened during the day, you might not like what happens. "Tech can give your children more information that you can, and it doesn't have your values," notes Dr. Steiner-Adair. "It won't be sensitive to your child's personality, and it won't answer his question in a developmentally appropriate way."

In addition, Dr. Wick advises delaying the age of first use as much as possible. "I use the same advice here that I use when talking about kids and alcohol—try to get as far as you can without anything at all." If your child is on Facebook, Dr. Wick says that you should be your child's friend and monitor her page. But she advises against going through text messages unless there is cause for concern. "If you have a reason to be worried then okay, but it better be a good reason. I see parents who are just plain old spying on their kids. Parents should begin by trusting their children. To not even give your kid the benefit of the doubt is incredibly damaging to the relationship. You have to feel like your parents think you're a good kid."

Offline, the gold standard advice for helping kids build healthy self-esteem is to get them involved in something that they're interested in. It could be sports or music or taking apart computers or volunteering—anything that sparks an interest and gives them confidence. When kids learn to feel good about what they can *do* instead of how they look and what they own, they're happier and better prepared for success in real life. That most of these activities also involve spending time interacting with peers face-to-face is just the icing on the cake.

Rachel Ehmke is a senior editor at the Child Mind Institute.

Peg Streep  **NO**

4 Things Teens Want and Need from Social Media

The superimportant, life-defining Facebook Like

Two girls—it turns out they are both eleven—are standing at the corner of 72nd Street and First Avenue. One is talking and the other is looking down at her phone, scrolling, and even though the light hasn't changed, she steps off the curb and starts crossing. I see the taxi out of the corner of my eye, barreling through the intersection and, more reflexively than not, I grab her by the shirt and pull her back. It all happens in seconds. After I introduce myself, I switch into mother-mode, asking whether her mom has told her not to text while she's crossing (she has) and what she was doing that was so important.

She was checking her Facebook. Technically, she's not old enough to be on Facebook, but never mind that. She explains that she was so busy Snapchatting that she probably hadn't checked Facebook in several hours—hence the urgency. It's astonishing to think that only nine years ago Facebook was in its first incarnation—in a dorm room at Harvard—but that now, it and other social media are inextricably part of the experience of growing up, as a recent Pew Research Center Study showed.

Other inventions—photography, the automobile, the telephone—changed both how people interact and how they viewed themselves, but the rise of social media seems to do so in ways that are both explicit and subtle at once. For one thing, the number of hours spent on social media is, in and of itself, noteworthy. How, in the end, this will shape the development of the young remains to be seen, but the four things teens and tweens want from social media are worth looking at. They tell us a lot about growing up digital.

1. To Get Attention

Information sharing is at the heart of getting attention for yourself and, according to Pew Research, teens are sharing plenty of it. 92 percent use their real names and just about the same number post photos of themselves. 71 percent post the name of their school and town. More than half post their e-mail. 84 percent post their interests and 82 percent their birthdays. Roughly one-quarter post videos of themselves. All of these percentages are higher—many of them significantly—since the last study the Pew Center did in 2006.

How benign is all this sharing? Well, it depends on your point of view. While only 9 percent of the teens surveyed worried about privacy (they thought they had a handle on it), recent research by Michal Kosinski, David Stillwell, and Thore Graepel demonstrated that using the Facebook Likes of 58,000 volunteers, they could accurately infer a variety of personal attributes. If you think about it, that's not really surprising. I happen to know the people I connect to on Facebook in the main, but if I look hard at what they post about, what they "like," and their photos, I could come up with a pretty detailed description of them which would include their political affiliations and opinions, their hobbies, attitudes etc. That puts another spin on the issue of what, in today's world, constitutes private information. 60 percent of teens keep their Facebooks private; 25 percent have a partly private profile; and 14 percent use public settings. But keep in mind that a quarter of tweens also have Twitter accounts—another fount of information.

Teens complain all the time about oversharing while they're sharing too much themselves. But if getting attention trumps all, will these kids ever learn how to set boundaries? The evidence, as you'll see, suggests not.

2. To Get Approval

The need to get peer approval isn't anything new, of course, but it used to take place largely in a real-world context; today, getting "approval" is closely associated with Facebook, especially with the "Like" feature which, the Pew Center researchers note, is a "strong proxy for social status so that Facebook users will manipulate their profiles and timeline content in order to garner the maximum number of 'likes.'" Teens will change out photos that have gotten too few likes and edit posts that don't garner approval.

Interestingly enough, while you might think that the more Facebook "friends" you have—the median for teens is 300—the less peer approval you might need, the opposite is true. In fact, researchers found that the more friends a teen had on Facebook—say 600 or more—the likelier he or she was to share more information and spend more time managing, curating, and editing his or her profile, photos, and posts. And the more friends you have actually increases the number of times you check in on Facebook. Not surprisingly, you're more likely to have a Twitter account if you have more Facebook friends too.

This phenomenon is explained by research done by Coye Cheshire that confirms that the "intrinsic satisfaction" derived from the popularity of something you've contributed—the sharing of information—actually increases your desire to share more in the future. If you get enough positive feedback, you'll be more inclined to share more and go out on a limb more the next time. In the same way, wanting to give social approval to someone else's sharing is going to motivate you to click that Like icon even more often.

This explains a lot about teen behavior online which often seems impulsive and thoughtless; it may not be.

Why Likes are so important is conveyed by what one fifteen-year-old girl said in a Pew focus group: "I think something that really changed for me in high school with Facebook is Facebook is really about popularity. And the popularity you have on Facebook transmits into the popularity you have in life." Bad diction aside, it's a sobering thought. And then there's this, uttered by another fifteen-year-old: "And there's something that we call 'like whores' because it's like people who desperately need 'likes' so there are a couple of things they do. First is post a picture at a prime time. And I'm not going to lie, I do that, too."

It's one thing to live in a world where Facebook Likes are essential to the marketing of almost everything and everyone—from books and authors, movies and songs, retail stores or museums—but is it healthy to have adolescents marketing themselves in the same way? Is this what our kids should want?

Is the goal to rival these Facebook page Likes? 301,000 (Psychology Today). 131,000 (Judy Blume). 2,585,000 (Paula Deen, and that was today.)

3. Cultivate an Image

In their focus groups, the Pew researchers found that a large number of teens complained about the burden of having to deal with Facebook—snooping parents, drama, and the work of curating the online persona, paying attention to all those Likes—but they all felt it was crucial nonetheless. As one researcher, Zeynep Tufekci wrote in her 2008 study, while adults and other commentators are confounded by what young people share online, they don't understand that "The kids want to be seen." The culture of social media values being seen over being known. In a social world that's mediated by technology, "being seen by those we wish to be seen by, in ways we wish to be seen, and thereby engaging in identity expression, communication, and impression management are central motivations." While her study focused on college students, it's clear that teens are well aware of and savvy about "impression management"; indeed, it appears to be their primary motivation.

4. Stay in the Loop and in the Game

I've written about FOMO—Fear of Missing Out—and like the 11-year-old crossing the street, teens worry a lot about being out of the loop. Since teens actually see Facebook and other social media as an extension of their physical universe—hence being popular on Facebook is an extension or validation of popularity in the real world—the idea of not participating or withdrawing is social suicide. That accounts for why teens complain about the "drama" on social media and continue to participate anyway.

Visitors to the Oracle at Delphi saw the words "Know Thyself" first. Would the Oracle today have a sign that said "Like Me" instead?

PEG STREEP, author or coauthor of 11 books, received her BA in English with Highest Honors from the University of Pennsylvania in 1969, where she was a Woodrow Wilson Fellow, a Magna Cum Laude inductee and a Phi Beta Kappa member. In 1971, she received her MA and MPhil with Highest Honors in English from Columbia University.

EXPLORING THE ISSUE

Is Social Media Use Detrimental to Teens?

Critical Thinking and Reflection

1. What are some of the ways that teenagers use social media?
2. What are some of the dangers of social media use that researchers warn about?
3. As technology and its accessibility continues to progress, what are some guidelines that you would recommend that parents implement in order to protect their children?

Is There Common Ground?

Raising adolescents these days is a complicated proposition, and parents or other adults often struggle to understand them, and to help them to understand what is best for them. In the grand scheme of things, social media is a new frontier that we are just beginning to research and really understand. There are tremendous benefits to having a social network at our fingertips, but there are also inherent dangers.

It would seem that it is especially difficult to set adequate limits for teenagers because adults also use social media (do as I say, not as I do), and therefore, they may not be as aware of the impact that it can have on younger brains or to perceive it as a dangerous thing to do. Finding the balance between the positive and negative impacts of social media on teens will take time, and is even more challenging given the ever-changing nature of technology. However, the more we can understand how social media effects the brain, the better prepared we can be to mitigate negative impacts on our most vulnerable of populations.

Additional Resources

"American Girls: Social Media and the Secret Lives of Teenagers" by Nancy Jo Sales (2017).

"A Parent's Guide to Understanding Social Media: Helping Your Teenager Navigate Life Online" by Mark Oestreicher & Adam McLane (2012).

"It's Complicated: the social lives of networked teens" by Danah Boyd (2015).

Internet References . . .

Facebook, Instagram, and Social Media

https://www.commonsensemedia.org/social-media/age/teens

Influence of social media on teenagers

http://www.huffingtonpost.com/suren-ramasubbu/influence-of-social-media-on-teenagers_b_7427740.html

Teens: This is how social media effects your brain.

http://www.cnn.com/2016/07/12/health/social-media-brain/index.html